Henry VII

Tony Imperato

Series Historical Consultant:
Dr R. A. H. Robinson,
The University of Birmingham

Stanley Thornes (Publishers) Ltd

First published in 1999 by:
Stanley Thornes (Publishers) Ltd
Ellenborough House
Wellington Street
CHELTENHAM GL50 1YW
England

99 00 01 02 03 / 10 9 8 7 6 5 4 3 2 1

A catalogue record for this book is available from the British Library.

ISBN 0-7487-4308-1

Illustrated by Davide Provenzale
Picture research by Christina Morgan
Typeset by Tech-Set Ltd, Gateshead, Tyne and Wear
Printed and bound in Great Britain by Redwood Books, Trowbridge, Wiltshire

Acknowledgements

With thanks to the following for permission to reproduce photographs and other copyright material in this book:

The Fotomas Index, 25, 37, 39, 49
National Portrait Gallery, 6 (top), 23, 47
Public Record Office, 32
Philip Sauvain, 20
Victoria and Albert Museum Picture Library, 6 (bottom)

Every effort has been made to contact copyright holders. The publishers apologise to anyone whose rights have been inadvertently overlooked, and will be happy to rectify any errors or omissions.

Contents

How to Use this Book

History at A-level is a more complex and demanding subject than at any preceding level, and it is with these new and higher demands on students in mind that the Pathfinder History series has been written. The basic aim of the book is simple: to enable you to appreciate the important issues that underpin understanding of Henry VII's reign as King of England.

What this book does not do is provide a single source of answers needed for exam success. The very nature of A-Level study demands that you use a range of resources in order to build up the understanding of different interpretations of issues, and in order to develop your own argument on exam topics. Pathfinder can make this subject more accessible by defining the key issues, giving an initial understanding of them and helping students to define questions for further investigation. It concentrates on the fundamentals surrounding Henry VII's impact on British history; the important issues, events and other characters of his period that you must understand, and which the examiners will want to see that you know.

Pathfinder, therefore, becomes more of a guide book to the subject. It can be used whenever you want within the A-level course: as an introduction; as a reminder or revision text; or throughout the course each time a new topic is started. Pathfinder also has several important features to help you get to grips with Henry VII and his times.

The book follows the three basic stages of the A-level process, explaining why they are important and why you are doing them. The three sections of the book are thus Overview, Enquiry and Investigation, and Review. These describe the three main methods of studying history at A-level. Therefore, when, for example, you answer a question on the seizure of power by Henry VII, you will recall why this book approaches this topic with these three headings in mind.

KEY ISSUES AND KEY SKILLS

Pathfinder is written around three basic principles. The first is that it covers the most important events, themes, ideas and concepts of the subject – the *Key Issues*. The second is that there are levels or tiers to these issues, so that a major question is broken down into its contributory questions and issues, making it easier to understand. And the third principle is that there are fundamental skills that you must develop and employ as historians at this level – the *Key Skills*.

These three principles combine in Section 1, where **The Big Picture** sets the whole scene of the topic and identifies the most important periods and events within the topic. Then, **The Key Issues** establishes what the author believes are the fundamental questions and answers to the subject as a whole, and examines these in more detail by raising contributory questions out of the main question. (Each period is discussed in more detail in Section 2: you will see page references for the appropriate chapter in each case.) Each period, therefore, has its own issues and concepts, providing a second tier of Key Issues. Finally, **What to Read, How to Read, Where to Find it and How to Use it** is a writing and researching section that offers hints and advice on the active study skills you will be using in A-level history.

The main focus of the book is Section 2, called **Enquiry and Investigation** because this is exactly what you are being asked to do most of the time during the A-level process. You are making historical enquiries and learning how to interpret sources and information every time you look at a document, analyse a photograph or read a topic. Each chapter takes as its title one of the periods identified in The Big Picture, and each one also identifies what you need to bear in mind when working on that particular issue or theme.

There is a useful tab at the start of each double-page spread which summarises the most important aspects of the topic and identifies the skills you will need to use when studying it. These are Key Skills, although you could think of them as key study skills if you prefer.

There are a number of Key Skills. They can be grouped together under the following headings with these definitions:

Skills for collecting information from historical sources

- Analysis: breaking down information into component parts (for example, making notes under section headings).

- Interpretation: considering the implications of information and cross-referencing to other sources or contextual knowledge in order to develop your understanding further. (Skills used within this are actually inference, deduction, extrapolation, interpolation, recall and synthesis.)
- Evaluation: assessing the validity of sources and the implications for the reliability of the information that they provide.
- Recording: arranging information into sections that allow easy retrieval when required – for example, making linear notes (good for large amounts of information), diagrams and flow charts or mind maps (good for establishing relationships between sections of information).

Skills for applying and using information

- Explanation: using information to show how and why something happened.
- Assessment: weighing up possible explanations or interpretations.
- Forming hypotheses: setting up an explanation or judgement for further testing.
- Testing hypotheses: using information to support and challenge a hypothesis in order to improve it.
- Setting a thesis: using the information to present, support and sustain a tested hypothesis and explanation of historical processes.

You will see that some skills are flagged more often than others, and there may be others, such as chronology, that are not defined here. However, the important point to remember is that these are the skills that the A-level historian has to have available for use, and that you are actually using them all the time already. The aim is to reinforce these skills for you, and to enable you to see how you are using them and why.

Section 3: Review then brings all the interpretations, investigations and issues that you have looked at to do with Henry VII into one place. **Synthesis** is the bringing together of issues, arguments and judgements into overall answers. It also poses answers as to what the author considered to be the main issues identified in Section 1. **Argument** then takes the information and hypotheses and applies them to more detailed essay questions and answers – of the style that you might find, and that you might write, in the exam. The **Final Review** is something of the author's own thoughts and conclusions on the subject at a broad level.

MARGINS AND ICONS

Pathfinder divides material as part of its strategy to focus attention on the most important issues. Therefore, the main central narrative discusses and interprets information but, although detailed, it cannot provide all the information on its topic. It must be integrated and supplemented with more detailed works, articles and documents.

All other sorts of information appear in the margins and you will see the following icons used alongside them. Not all icons appear in every chapter, and some chapters have other features included as well, but the icons should help you manage the extra information given on topics:

Documents, historiography and sources – quotes from texts, individuals and passages

Suggested headings for notes

Suggested further reading

Sample activities and exam-style questions

General hints, study tips and advice

Key words

Henry VII, by Michael Sittow

This book is a history of the reign of Henry VII, England's first Tudor monarch. Henry tends to be overshadowed by his more famous son, Henry VIII, and his grand-daughter, Elizabeth I, but they probably could not have achieved as much as they did without the foundations that he laid. During his reign, he brought much needed stability back to England after a long period of conflict and revived the fortunes of the Crown. The next four pages provide a brief account of what Henry did to achieve these things. They will give you an overview, or as the title says, The Big Picture.

The Big Picture: the Reign of Henry VII

HOW HENRY BECAME KING (SEE PAGES 14–17)

- In the late fifteenth century, England saw a struggle for control of the throne between the Lancastrians, who had ruled since 1399, and the Yorkists, who were unhappy at the misgovernment at home and failure in wars abroad.
- Henry was a member of the House of Tudor, related to the Lancastrians. He spent the first 14 years of his life in his Welsh homeland, a victim of the political manoeuvring between the Lancastrians and Yorkists. When the Yorkist king Edward IV finally secured the throne, Henry fled into exile abroad.
- Edward IV's death in 1483 led to the swift seizure of power by his brother Richard III. His unpopular reign drew support to Henry's side.
- Henry launched an invasion in 1485. His army met Richard's at Bosworth Field in the Midlands and won, killing Richard and allowing Henry to take the crown.

ENGLAND IN 1485 (SEE PAGES 18–21)

- England was a rural country with few large towns. Its population had been reduced by the Black Death over a century earlier and was only just beginning to recover.
- Most people made their living through agriculture, but the woollen industry was an important source of jobs, money and exports.
- The Crown was the most important political institution, although kings did not have unlimited control. In theory, they had wide-ranging powers; but in practice, they depended on the support and co-operation of leading subjects to use them.
- Government was based on the royal household and exercised through specialised departments and councils. Parliament was useful in passing laws and raising taxation, but had occasionally challenged the king's powers.
- Defeat in the Hundred Years War, the problems that Henry VII faced as a new and untried king, and changes in other European monarchies meant that England was eclipsed as a major power by France and Spain.

A bust of Henry VII, by Torrigiano

DEFEATING PRETENDERS (SEE PAGES 22–25)

- Henry moved quickly to establish his hold on the country, by ensuring legal recognition of his actions and by neutralising his enemies.
- Disaffected nobles and foreign rulers who were eager to keep Henry weak and distracted gathered around 'pretenders'.
- Both Lambert Simnel and Perkin Warbeck were encouraged to pose as the rightful heir to the throne, and won enough support in their bases abroad to threaten the stability of Henry's kingdom.
- Even though Henry defeated both of these rebellions against him, he remained afraid of further challenges for the rest of his reign.

CONTROLLING THE NOBILITY (SEE PAGES 26–29)

- Henry was aware that the major families who made up the nobility could be a serious threat to his power. They controlled large areas of land, were wealthy enough to have their own armies and held political power in government and the administration.
- However, Henry recognised that the nobility performed important functions that helped to ensure good government.
- He followed a careful balancing act in dealing with his nobles, rewarding loyalty to him while restricting their numbers and prospects of advancement.
- Financial controls, such as bonds and recognisances, and legal controls, such as laws against illegal retaining, were also used to force their obedience.

IMPROVING FINANCES (SEE PAGES 30–33)

- Henry has gained a reputation as a shrewd financial manager.
- He was successful in restoring royal revenues and left the Crown in a healthy financial position at the end of his reign.
- He exploited the range of possible sources of income to the full, while keeping the Crown from becoming a hostage to either Parliament or the nobility, both of which he depended on for revenue.
- To manage his wealth, he improved the machinery of government that dealt with collecting, spending and auditing income.

What was Henry VII like?

The most famous description of Henry's appearance and personality is given by Polydore Vergil in *Anglicae Historia*. Vergil was an Italian diplomat who came to England in 1502 on behalf of the Pope and was asked by Henry VII to write a history of England. His account is said to be reliable because Vergil knew Henry personally, and also because he did not complete the book until after Henry's death, so had less reason to be deliberately flattering:

'His body was slender, but well built and strong; his height above the average. His appearance was remarkably attractive and his face was cheerful, especially when speaking; his eyes were small and blue, his teeth few, poor and blackish; his hair was thin and white; his complexion sallow.

'His spirit was distinguished, wise and prudent; his mind was brave and resolute and never, even at moments of the greatest danger, deserted him. In government he was shrewd and prudent, so that no one dared to get the better of him by guile or deceit. He was gracious and kind and was as attentive to his visitors as he was easy of access. His hospitality was splendidly generous.

'He was most fortunate in war, although he was more inclined to peace. He cherished justice above all things. He was the most ardent supporter of our faith, but all these virtues were obscured latterly by avarice.'

This book is not a biography of Henry VII, so it does not chart his reign chronologically. Instead, it focuses on important aspects and themes that will run throughout your study of English history, such as the monarch's relationship with the nobility or the Crown's finances. The advantage of looking at Henry's reign in this way is that you can build up ideas and information that will help to create paragraphs in examination essays. The disadvantage is that it can be difficult to see how one event or change triggered something else in a different aspect of his reign. Drawing up a timeline of key events is a useful way of solving this problem.

Using The Big Picture

The aim of this section is to give you a key-point summary of the main themes of Henry's reign. As you begin to study Henry's reign in more depth, it will allow you to form a quick overview of what you need to know. However, you can also use The Big Picture throughout your course to remind yourself about basic ideas and information and, in final revision, it is a useful checklist of the areas that an examiner might expect you to cover.

STRENGTHENING ROYAL GOVERNMENT (SEE PAGES 34–37)

- England had an effective system of national and local government that had developed over a number of centuries.
- Henry saw the restoration of strong government as essential to his survival as king and set about revitalising the institutions of central government, especially those within the royal household.
- The approach to government in different parts of the country, such as Ireland and the North, was dictated by local circumstances, but Henry was always careful to neutralise any opposition. In local government, he strengthened the work of Justices of the Peace.
- Henry relied on loyal advisers and professional administrators, and curbed the influence of major noble families and Parliament.

DEVELOPING TRADE AND COMMERCE (SEE PAGES 38–41)

- The domestic economy was firmly based on agriculture and the woollen industry. Both had been changing in the century leading up to 1485 and posed different challenges for the government to master.
- Henry attempted to protect English imports and exports through Navigation Acts that regulated the carrying of goods and by signing treaties with countries that were major markets.
- Henry encouraged the expansion of trade with more countries and principalities, such as Spain and Florence, but he found it more difficult to penetrate markets in northern Europe.
- He also saw opportunities in the plans of John and Sebastian Cabot to search for a westward route to the spice markets of the Far East, and he helped to finance their voyages of discovery.

MANAGING FOREIGN POLICY (SEE PAGES 42–45)

- Lack of finances, the growth of a powerful French state and fears that his enemies might back rivals for the crown gave Henry good reasons to be cautious in his foreign policy.
- His reign coincided with a shift in the balance of power in Europe, away from Anglo-French rivalry and towards hostility between France and Spain. The main battleground in Europe also changed from northern Europe towards conflict over southern Europe, especially control of the Italian peninsula.
- Henry used diplomacy rather than warfare to achieve his goals, and was generally successful in keeping the peace with potential enemies. The major crisis of his reign arose over disputes about the future of Brittany.
- His foreign policy dealt with a wide range of countries: France, Spain, Burgundy, the Holy Roman Empire, the principalities of northern Italy, and Scotland.

HENRY'S LEGACY (SEE PAGES 46–49)

- By 1509, Henry had re-established an effective system of personal government, built on sound finances. He had restricted the influence of rival members of the ruling elite, such as the nobility and Parliament, and had mapped out a cautious but realistic approach to foreign policy.
- However, while the institution of the monarchy was undoubtedly strengthened, Henry's strict and grasping policies made him personally unpopular.
- Whether his achievements would continue to be developed depended on the personalities and interests of his successors. Henry VIII undid a number of key policies that his father had followed, but was reacting as much to the new realities of the sixteenth century as he was against any weaknesses that Henry VII had left him.

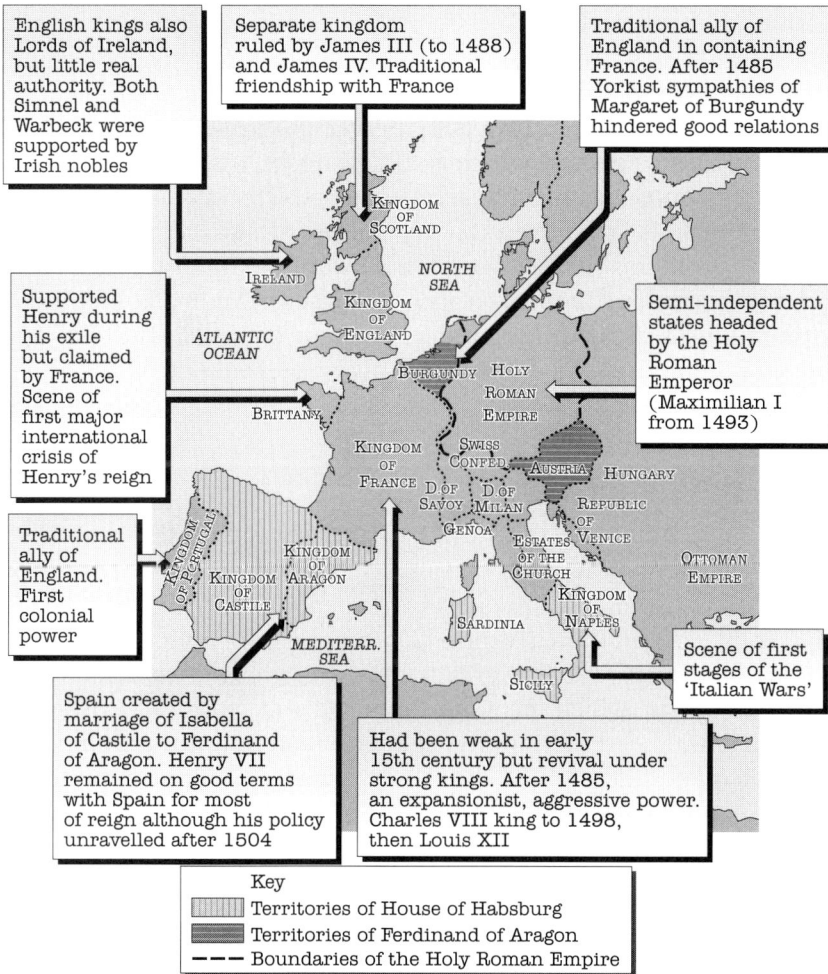

English kings also Lords of Ireland, but little real authority. Both Simnel and Warbeck were supported by Irish nobles

Separate kingdom ruled by James III (to 1488) and James IV. Traditional friendship with France

Traditional ally of England in containing France. After 1485 Yorkist sympathies of Margaret of Burgundy hindered good relations

Supported Henry during his exile but claimed by France. Scene of first major international crisis of Henry's reign

Semi-independent states headed by the Holy Roman Emperor (Maximilian I from 1493)

Traditional ally of England. First colonial power

Spain created by marriage of Isabella of Castile to Ferdinand of Aragon. Henry VII remained on good terms with Spain for most of reign although his policy unravelled after 1504

Had been weak in early 15th century but revival under strong kings. After 1485, an expansionist, aggressive power. Charles VIII king to 1498, then Louis XII

Scene of first stages of the 'Italian Wars'

Key
- Territories of House of Habsburg
- Territories of Ferdinand of Aragon
- – – – Boundaries of the Holy Roman Empire

England and Europe in the late fifteenth century

Key dates and events in Henry VII's reign

1485	Henry becomes king after defeating Richard III at Battle of Bosworth Field
1486	Marriage to Elizabeth of York; Lovell's Rebellion
1487	Simnel's Rebellion; Battle of Stoke; birth of Prince Arthur
1488	Escalating crisis in Brittany
1489	Treaty of Medina del Campo with Spain; Yorkshire Rebellion
1491	Birth of Prince Henry; first appearance of Perkin Warbeck
1492	Settlement of the Breton Crisis
1494	Attempts to reform the government of Ireland
1496	Magnus Intercursus trade agreement with Burgundy; Henry finances Cabot's first voyage
1497	Cornish Rebellion
1499	Executions of Perkin Warbeck and the Earl of Warwick
1501	Marriage of Arthur to Catherine of Aragon
1502	Death of Arthur
1503	Death of Elizabeth of York
1509	Death of Henry VII, succession of his son Henry VIII

Using the map, list the countries that were likely to cause problems for Henry VII and those which were potential allies.

What are 'Key Issues'?

Key Issues are a way of studying history with a purpose. They pose questions about Henry's reign that will help you to shape and organise your research around relevant and important ideas and themes.

How to use the Key Issues

Key Issues are designed to help you to focus on what is important. In every chapter in Section 2, Key Issues have been posed to remind you of what to look for as you read. They do not pretend to be every single question that could usefully be asked of the topic—hopefully, you will think of questions of your own as you grow in confidence and knowledge. As with The Big Picture, these Key Issues can also help in revision. You could get someone else to ask you these questions, to check how well you have remembered and understood, or you could write revision notes answering each of them.

Areas of enquiry

You will see that four concerns dominate the questions on these pages: **aims, methods, success** and **effects**. These are all standard areas of historical enquiry that can be applied to the reigns of any ruler that you are studying, with the certainty that they are popular starting-points for exam questions.

The Key Issues

Historians ask different sorts of questions about the past. To begin with, they will try to reconstruct a sequence of events from the fragments of story contained in primary sources. In this case, their central concern is to ask 'who', 'when' and 'what'. These questions are useful to give you a good grounding of knowledge about the period, but will not be enough to help you write successful essays. Historians do not just collect facts about the past for their own sake; they ask questions about them – to construct patterns and interpretations that make sense of, and give order to, the jumble of detail that is lying around. It is interesting to know that something happened at a particular moment in the past; but making connections between events, by asking why something happened and what effects it had, creates a much deeper and more worthwhile understanding – and it is this that A-level is seeking to test.

Because Henry came to the throne at such a troubled time, historians have considered his reign in the context of how the monarchy developed and how it shaped English political institutions. This has created a debate, which is still going on, over the significance of his reign and his overall achievements. Historians have asked questions such as: What were Henry's aims? How successfully did he tackle the problems that he faced? What were the main characteristics of Henry's style and approach to government? Were his methods a continuation of those of his predecessors, or did he institute a more modern monarchy? And, because of this, was 1485 a turning-point in English history?

1. WHAT WERE HENRY'S AIMS?

The changes that took place in England between 1485 and 1509, which transformed it from a unruly, divided land into a firmly governed kingdom, were created by the energy and vision of Henry VII. It is important, then, to appreciate what Henry saw as his task and what goals he pursued. To a great extent, his aims were shaped by the circumstances in which he found himself – an untrained, untested monarch at the head of a country that had seen political instability for at least a generation. How did Henry's early life and experiences shape his aims? How did the condition of England in the late fifteenth century offer him opportunities to achieve his aims? And how did it present him with problems? Once installed as king, Henry applied himself to overcoming the weaknesses of his inheritance and to strengthening the Crown. What aims did he have with regard to the nobility, central government, rival claimants and finances, and how did he change the tone of English foreign policy? More generally, did he pursue these aims consistently throughout the reign, or were there periods when some dominated more than others? Were his policies those traditionally pursued by English kings? Does he deserve his reputation for realism and caution?

2. How Did Henry Pursue His Aims?

Until the 1970s, one of the most persistent claims about Henry VII was that he was a 'New Monarch', the first modern king who employed methods that were sharply different from those of his medieval predecessors. Since then, revisionist historians have widened our knowledge and understanding of the Yorkist period and in the process have emphasised continuities rather than changes. They have looked at the extent to which Henry VII's approach to managing finances, controlling the nobility, organising government, promoting trade and dealing with foreign powers simply reflected or extended Edward IV's methods. Did he use established methods or is there evidence of innovation and change? To what extent did the condition of England at the end of the fifteenth century dictate the methods he used? What was the balance between persuasion and coercion? Is it fair to describe him as 'ruthless', 'cautious' or 'opportunist'?

3. How Successful Was Henry?

Few doubt that Henry managed a remarkable achievement in simply being able to leave a peaceful kingdom and a respected Crown to his son. Yet there is a danger of accepting that fact uncritically. As well as asking what different achievements Henry had accomplished by 1509, what problems and failures remained? Had Henry really solved the 'problem of the nobility'? Was his foreign policy a resounding success? Did he ignore the interests of trade and the economy to pursue dynastic security? Had he moved England forward or merely restored what was already there? At the heart of these debates is the position of the Crown: How secure was it in the hands of the Tudors by 1509? How did events at the turn of the sixteenth century threaten Henry's achievements? If the Crown was stronger, why was Henry personally so unpopular?

4. What Was the Impact of Henry's Reign?

Within a long span of history, Henry's reign seems to mark something of a turning-point, finally ending the instability of fifteenth-century politics and paving the way for the powerful monarchies of the sixteenth. However, some writers have challenged the abruptness of this transformation and asked whether it is too convenient to see it as neatly coinciding with Henry VII's reign. What were the strengths and weaknesses of England by 1509? To what extent had Henry's policies laid the foundations of a strong dynasty? Did Henry VIII continue his father's policies in the early years of his reign? How did government and society continue to develop under the Later Tudors? Were these developments possible because of Henry VII, or were they caused by shifting circumstances?

Medieval or modern?

The central debate that has taken place about Henry VII is where to place him in relation to other rulers. Was he the first of England's 'modern' kings or the last of its 'medieval' monarchs? This is an issue that you will need to judge as you read about Henry's different policies and achievements. To help, the characteristics often used to distinguish modern from medieval include the following:

- a more professional approach to government, using trained officials and specialised councils
- a good financial framework
- strong institutions in central government, allowing the monarch's policies to be implemented effectively
- the limited influence of other members of the ruling elite, such as members of Parliament and the nobility

Revisionists – historians who challenge traditional interpretations of the past and who offer alternative ways of viewing a person, event or period. For example, historians traditionally emphasised 1485 as the starting-point for changes in the style and methods of government that created the powerful sixteenth-century Tudor state. Revisionist historians challenge this approach, arguing that there are rarely sudden or dramatic changes in history. They seek to demonstrate that Henry drew upon the work of his predecessors, causing the form of government to evolve rather than revolutionising it.

Reading around the subject

Successful study at A-level should involve reading around the subject, which means using a range of resources to piece together a clear and varied view of the topic. While the basic facts about Henry's reign might not vary much from book to book, the conclusions that writers draw from this information and the way in which they present material will. An awareness of a variety of opinions will allow you to form your own ideas and use them to enrich your discussions and essays.

Making notes

In *Learning History, a Guide to Advanced Study* (Macmillan, 1986), Richard Brown and Christopher Daniels give this advice about note-making:

'It is important to have two points clear when note-taking. First, notes are for you, nobody else. Although some notes may be examined, and sometimes marked, by your teachers they are part of your thinking and reflection on a particular subject. They should be written *only* for you as triggers and aids to learning. Secondly, there is little point in taking notes on anything unless they are solidly based on your understanding of that subject. Taking notes is a highly individual activity: whether the method used actually works is the only criterion of success.'

For more advice about effective study skills for history, see The *History Manual* by J. A. Cloake, V. Crinnon and S. M. Harrison (Framework Press, 1985) or the Brown and Daniels book mentioned above.

What to Read, How to Read, Where to Find it and How to Use it

1. WHERE TO FIND INFORMATION FOR YOURSELF

This book aims to give you a starting-point for your research on Henry VII by charting a route through the different aspects of his reign. However, it should not be the only text that you consult. To begin with, perhaps the most useful books are general histories of Tudor England, which will cover what happened between 1485 and 1509 in a chapter or so, and will usually give you information about earlier events such as the Wars of the Roses and reign of Edward IV. In most libraries, these are classified in section 942.05. Once you have built up some knowledge about the period, you could then consult the more specialist textbooks about Henry VII. Many of these are written for students and are divided into sections that are similar to those in this book, covering themes such as challenges to the throne, finances, relations with the nobility, foreign policy, trade and government. These textbooks on Henry VII will often take you further into the major debates about his reign. A third sort of text that you might wish to consult is biographies of Henry VII. You should not need to read a biography from cover to cover for A-level, but you might want to dip into some chapters or use the index to get more detail about particular events or developments in the reign. Such books can be found under the classification 942.051 in most libraries. Finally, articles in magazines such as *History Today* will give you the latest ideas and information about aspects of Henry VII's reign. Again, these might be too detailed for ordinary essays, but can be very useful for project work or just for general interest.

2. HOW TO DECIDE WHAT TO READ

Few students have the time to read a textbook from cover to cover, but this is rarely necessary anyway. The key to effective research lies in knowing what you want to find and then browsing texts to locate it. Early on in your study of a topic, you will probably *read for information* to get facts about who, what, when and where. However, as you become more familiar with the topic, *reading for ideas* should take over, to get writers' opinions about why and how. The Key Issues section in this book shows you the sorts of ideas to look for, but you should try to develop your own research questions as well.

In most of the chapters in Section 2, suggestions for particularly useful texts have been given to help you extend your reading. At the end of the book, on page 62, is a list of works that would be ideal next steps for research. Most have been written with a student audience in mind. You will find that they contain greater depth in their discussion of the themes of Henry's reign than this introductory book allows and are all good at providing precise examples to illustrate arguments and ideas. From these, you could graduate to books that deal with later medieval Britain, or to specialist articles and biographies.

3. HOW TO READ EFFICIENTLY

To get information quickly from a book, scan the contents page and identify the chapters that might be relevant – or, if you already have a more precise area to research, use the index. Don't start to make notes until you have an idea of how the section you want to use is organised. Writers sometimes make this easy by dividing chapters up into short sections, but if this has not been done, try reading just the first sentence or two of each paragraph to see what it is about. Alternatively, try 'skimming' a chapter as well: think of a key word that would show where there is relevant information (such as 'wool', if you are researching the domestic economy) and quickly scan each page to see if the word appears.

4. HOW TO MAKE EFFECTIVE NOTES

Note-making is a matter of personal taste and you need to find a style that suits you. Remember, though, that the purpose of note-making is to store the detailed information and ideas that you will find in a textbook in a clear, structured and more convenient format. If you are not very practised at note-making, the temptation will be to copy out chunks of books or write notes in a way that resembles this paragraph – just uninterrupted words on a page.

It is much better to develop alternatives that will divide up your notes into manageable sections that look attractive. In that way, you will be able to get at the information quickly, and revising the topic won't seem such a chore:

- Get organised. Buy a colourful ring-binder, decorate dividers with pictures of each monarch, choose stylish and comfortable pens in different colours and arm yourself with a highlighter and some correction fluid (such as Tippex).
- Use different colours, text sizes and writing styles to add variety, and paste in pictures and maps. Advertisers will tell you that the greater the visual impact, the more memorable it will be!
- Use subheadings, lists and bullet points like this to break up large blocks of information into their component parts.
- Draw flow charts, graphs and diagrams to summarise information and show connections.
- Experiment with the layout of your notes. Draw a wider margin, so that you can keep a summary alongside your main information, or use the left-hand side of pages in your ring-binder to collect arguments and essay ideas and the right-hand side for major facts.
- Remember that you will often want to add to your notes as you come across new information and ideas, so leave plenty of space in and around each section.

Using the Internet

Although you are looking at the fairly distant past, there is no reason why you should not use the most up-to-date technology. If you have never used the Internet before, think of it as a vast library of information, but without any visible organisation. Once you have logged on, you may know a particular 'address' (most begin with 'http://www.') and you may be able to get to a useful site immediately by typing it into the address box on the toolbar of your browser. This book does not suggest particular addresses simply because they often change, as web sites are taken off-line or people move to new service providers. Instead, use a search engine, such as Alta Vista, Lycos, Excite or Yahoo, and type in a key word or phrase: 'Battle of Bosworth Field', 'Henry VII' or 'Tudors' will all throw up a list of sites. Some (such as 'The Tudor Lodge Hotel'!) will be irrelevant, and many will be disappointing – just basic introductions or simple biographies – but there are some gems if you persevere. Remember to follow possible links and bookmark any useful sites.

Films

Henry VII has not attracted the attention of the film industry in the way that Richard III or the Later Tudors have. Since watching a film is probably better for getting a visual impression of the period than it is for finding facts, try any of the films dealing with the fifteenth and sixteenth centuries, such as the classic 1955 version of Shakespeare's *King Richard III*, starring Laurence Olivier, or the 1998 film *Elizabeth*, about the life of Elizabeth I.

THE KEY ISSUE

How did the events of 1457–1470 help to advance Henry's claim to the throne?

THE KEY SKILLS

Chronology: building an account of events
Explanation: identifying causes

WHAT YOU HAVE TO DO

There are two sorts of information given here – biographical details about Henry and background material on political problems of the time. You might find it useful to draw up a chart of Henry's early life, but it is more important to list the ways in which the political background might have helped (or hindered) any claim to the throne.

Henry's Early Life, 1457–1470

Few contemporaries knew much about Henry, let alone thought that he might become king. Henry was 28 when he became king, but he had spent the first 14 years of his life away from the centre of political activity and the next 14 in exile, first in Brittany and then in France. He had received no training in kingship and had been carried to the throne as much by luck as by judgement.

To understand why Henry, the man Richard III called the 'unknown Welshman', was able to seize the crown in 1485 you need to look at:

● how the rivalry between and within major families threatened each of the kings who ruled during Henry's lifetime, and determined the course of events
● Henry's slender claim to the throne, and how it became stronger over the years as better placed rivals died, and
● how Henry prepared the ground for his takeover

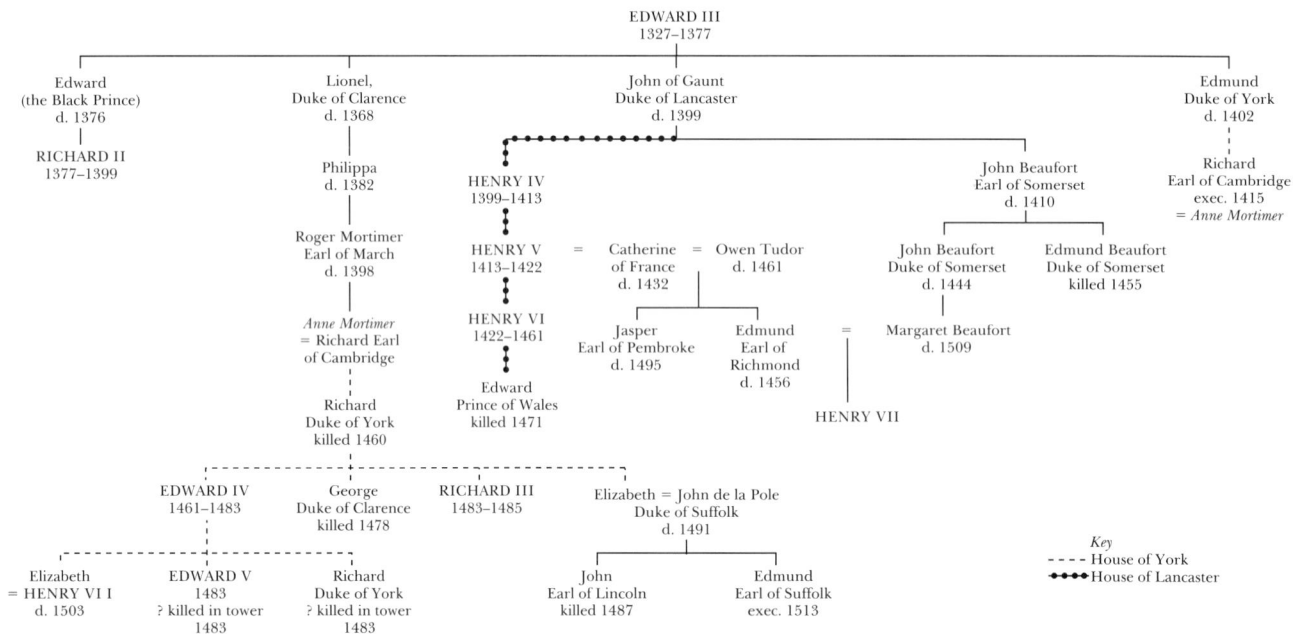

The Houses of Lancaster and York. The intermarriage of different branches of Edward III's family elevated the ambitions of leading nobles and so set up the conditions for the political instability of the mid-fifteenth century.

Family trees

Don't ignore family trees! After all, monarchs and nobles went to great lengths to extend their dynastic connections. You can use the family tree to see why Henry's claim was weak (it came through the female line) and who else might have harboured designs on the crown in 1485.

HENRY'S FAMILY

The Tudors were an offshoot from the main Lancastrian dynasty that had taken control of the crown from 1399. The Lancastrian kings were Henry IV (1399–1413), Henry V (1413–1422) and Henry VI (1422–1461 and 1470–1471). Henry's grandfather, Owen Tudor, had been a member of Henry V's court who had been steadily promoted and, after the death of the king, had secretly married his widow. Their eldest son was Edmund Tudor, the Earl of Richmond. Edmund had married Margaret Beaufort, who was a descendant of an earlier king, Edward III. Edmund and Margaret's only son was Henry Tudor. These intermarriages between noble houses gave Henry a distant claim to the throne, but there were doubts about the legitimacy of his family, so no one expected anything to come of this. His claim rested on a link that stretched back four generations, and there were sufficient men with better pedigrees and closer ties to the House of Lancaster than the unknown Henry Tudor.

THE LAST YEARS OF HENRY VI'S REIGN 1457–1461

Henry VII was born in January 1457. His father had been captured by the Yorkist enemies of Henry VI and had died in prison a couple of months before Henry was born, so Edmund's brother, Jasper Tudor, took care of both the 13-year-old widow and her new-born son at his castle at Pembroke in Wales.

At that time, the Lancastrian king Henry VI ruled England. However, his reign was rapidly spinning out of control. England had ruled large areas of France in the Middle Ages but, under Henry VI's disastrous foreign policies, had lost everything except Calais by 1453. This failure to protect his inheritance had helped to push Henry into a nervous breakdown in 1453–1454, and he continued to suffer bouts of what was possibly schizophrenia for the rest of his life. This weakness at the centre of power encouraged the ambitions of the major nobles. Henry had unwisely favoured a select group within his household, and resentment at the lands and favours he had showered on them built up, especially among the family and supporters of his cousin, the Duke of York. While Henry Tudor was still a small child, the Duke of York and the Earl of Warwick raised an army and toppled Henry VI from the throne.

EDWARD IV'S FIRST REIGN 1461–1470

In 1461, Edward IV became king and began the brief period of rule by the House of York. Because Jasper Tudor had been a loyal supporter of Henry VI, his castle was seized and four-year-old Henry was placed in the care of its new owner, William Herbert. Henry Tudor's future seemed predetermined: he would be raised in Wales and would probably marry William Herbert's daughter. A life of obscurity among the minor nobility beckoned. Again, though, the political manoeuvring that was going on within the nobility was to change everything. Although Edward IV had become king, little else was settled. Henry VI and his wife still lived, and Lancastrian nobles still held scattered lands across England, from which they could plot rebellion. Worse, the friendship between Edward and the Earl of Warwick that had won the throne broke down in the 1460s to the extent that Warwick plotted to overthrow Edward and allow Henry VI back to power.

Who's who?

If you are just beginning your study of Tudor England, the procession of kings who feature in the story of Henry's early life can seem bewildering. Use the quick summaries in this chapter to keep up with them!

Henry IV
Lancastrian King of England, 1399–1413. Originally Henry Bolingbroke, cousin of Richard II. He became king when he and a group of nobles overthrew Richard. He had a troubled early reign, dogged by criticism from self-confident Parliaments and rebellions against his seizure of power.

Henry V
Lancastrian King of England, 1413–1422. A well-regarded figure who led England to great victories in the Hundred Years War against France, at Agincourt in 1415 and Rouen in 1419.

Henry VI
Lancastrian King of England, 1422–1461 and 1470–1471. He inherited the crown aged three, so there was long regency in which leading nobles jostled for position. After he came of age, a generally unsuccessful reign was marked by heavy losses in France, unruly nobles, unhappy Parliaments and a final descent into madness. Kinder interpretations suggest that he was unfortunate to rule at a time when England was beginning to be eclipsed by France.

- How many people had better claims to the throne than Henry?
- What happened to each of them?

Do some research to find the answers.

The Path to the Crown, 1471–1485

Edward IV was overthrown in 1470 and Henry VI returned for a second reign. This was to be very short, however, because Edward quickly mustered support abroad and returned, killing the Earl of Warwick and Henry's only son in the brief, bloody battle to recapture the crown. Once reinstalled as king, Edward IV dealt with Henry VI, almost certainly ordering his murder in the Tower of London. All of this had an alarming effect on the 14-year-old Henry Tudor. The deaths of Henry VI and his son wiped out the main line of the House of Lancaster and significantly advanced his own claim to the throne. From being a distant child of a minor family, Henry Tudor had now become a potential threat to Edward IV. Recognising this, Henry fled to Brittany, where he became a political refugee for the next 14 years.

EXILE 1471–1485

At home, Edward IV began to revive government after the chaos of Henry VI's later years and the destructive in-fighting among the nobility. While he faced no real threat from the House of Lancaster, the scheming of his brothers meant that instability had not yet ended. When Edward died in 1483, his youngest brother Richard, the Duke of Gloucester, moved quickly to seize the throne for himself. Edward had helped to create this situation by rewarding Richard with the lands of the Earl of Warwick, which had given him a massive power base in the Midlands and the North, but everyone was surprised by the ruthlessness that Richard showed. Edward had two sons, both children, who were better claimants to the throne than Richard. In one of the most infamous incidents in British history, Richard is said to have had the two princes murdered in the Tower of London, so that his path to the throne would be clear.

PREPARATIONS 1483–1485

The deaths of Edward IV and his sons again advanced the position of the exiled Henry Tudor. For noblemen unhappy at Richard III's actions, Henry now seemed to be an excellent alternative. The Duke of Buckingham – who had been one of Richard's closest supporters – wrote to Henry, encouraging him to invade England and take the crown. Henry launched his first attack from Brittany in autumn 1483, while Buckingham and his allies rebelled at home. It was a disaster, but Henry escaped capture and soon found that more and more of Richard's enemies – including some major players, such as the Lancastrian Earl of Oxford – were arriving at his court in exile. Henry made a shrewd political gesture on Christmas Day 1483 by declaring that if he became king he would marry Elizabeth of York, the daughter of Edward IV. This would unite the warring houses of York and Lancaster, and it emphasised that he wanted to be associated with the branch of the family that had lost the crown to the 'usurper' Richard III.

THE KEY ISSUE

Why was Henry able to seize the crown in 1485?

THE KEY SKILLS

Chronology: building an account of events

Explanation: identifying causes

WHAT YOU HAVE TO DO

Use pages 14–17 to identify the stages by which Henry moved closer to the crown. Then think more widely about why Henry was able to become king. This should involve consideration of his strengths and his enemies' weaknesses, long- and short-term factors and whether, as suggested in the account, his eventual victory was 'as much by luck as by judgement'.

Shakespeare's view of Bosworth

In *King Richard III* (Act V, Scene IV), Shakespeare makes reference to Richard's difficulty in identifying Henry in the midst of the battle:

King Richard: Slave! I have set my life upon a cast,

And I will stand the hazard of the die.

I think there be six Richmonds in the field;

Five have I slain to-day, instead of him.–

A horse, A horse! my kingdom for a horse!'

Given that the king had this problem, it is not hard to imagine how little known Henry was in 1485, or why pretenders could so easily claim to be leading contenders for the crown and be accepted.

The Seizure of the Crown 1485

Henry continued to prepare for a full-blown invasion. While reports and intelligence poured in through English visitors, he wrote to possible allies in Wales and England, arguing his claim to the throne. Richard took Henry's activities seriously and made an attempt to seize him when the Duke of Brittany fell ill early in 1485, but Henry escaped to France, where he negotiated military help from King Charles VIII. With this support, Henry risked another invasion. On 1 August 1485, his small fleet of ships set sail from France; they landed on the Welsh coast a week later. Henry quickly marched into England, gathering support as he went. He met Richard at the Battle of Bosworth Field on 22 August. Even in the battle, Henry could not be certain of victory. He had not attracted a massive groundswell of public support, had never led an army into battle before, and went in with an army that was probably only about half the size of Richard's. It was the decision of the Stanley family, midway through the battle, to commit their army to Henry's side that swayed the outcome in Henry's favour. At the end, Richard was dead and, to the surprise of many people, Henry was king.

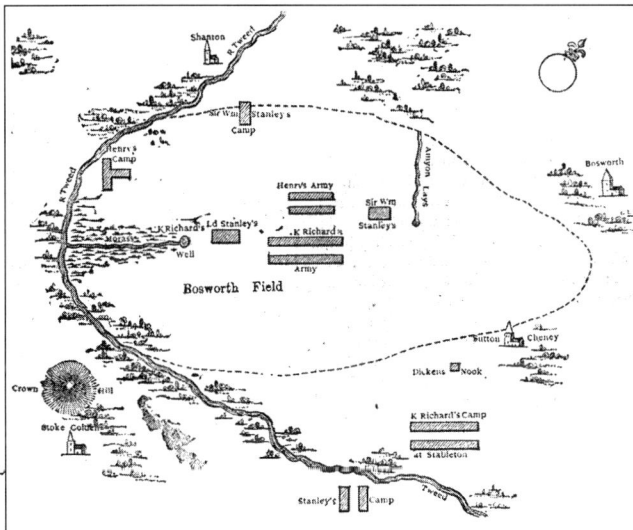

The Battle of Bosworth Field

This map supposedly shows what was happening on 22 August 1485. Although it is one of the most famous battles fought on English soil, very little is known for certain about what went on at Bosworth Field. This is because no one who was there on the day recorded the events, so that all 'primary' accounts are actually later reconstructions. Even eyewitnesses would have had a difficult job to describe accurately the sequence of events and what was happening around each of the leaders in the midst of the battlefield chaos. Since Bosworth, writers have disagreed about many of the facts of the battle, such as:

- how many noblemen were present at the battle
- whether Henry won because Richard's forces deserted their king, or whether it was because Richard engaged Henry's forces too soon
- whether the Earl of Northumberland deliberately stayed on the sidelines, betraying Richard, or whether he could not participate anyway because his army was wrongly positioned
- whether the battle was even fought at Bosworth – some think that the real location was near the town of Dadlington, a mile and a half away

Who's who?

Edward IV
Yorkist King of England, 1461–1470 and 1471–1483. The son of Richard, Duke of York, who had been named as heir by Henry VI. He took the crown by force with the aid of the Earl of Warwick (the 'Kingmaker'). His first reign was marked by miscalculation and a struggle to maintain loyalty, but his second reign was more successful and laid the foundations of government that Henry VII was to build on.

Richard III
Yorkist King of England, 1483–1485. The subject of extreme opinions, ranging from the hunchbacked tyrant of Tudor propaganda to the sympathetic image of a successful but unfortunate ruler, portrayed by the modern Richard III Society. Whatever his personal qualities, his actions had alienated enough key people by 1485 to allow Henry his opportunity.

Does all this uncertainty and disagreement about the circumstances of the Battle of Bosworth Field matter?

Create a timeline of the important events from 1457 to 1485. Put in blocks to show the reign of each king before Henry VII. Draw the timeline to scale, so that you can see easily when the periods of greatest activity were. As you read more about Henry's reign itself, you could then extend the timeline to show what else Henry did to make his victory secure.

How might Henry's experiences before 1485 have affected his behaviour as king?

THE KEY ISSUES

- How was England governed in the late fifteenth century?
- How powerful was the Crown within the system of government?

THE KEY SKILLS

Empathy: appreciating the conditions of a different age
Interpretation: deciding on the relevance and usefulness of information
Selection: choosing information to present an argument
Evaluation: reaching an overall judgement

WHAT YOU HAVE TO DO

Essays will not ask you directly about the state of Henry's kingdom, but this section provide useful backgrou information and a start   t for comparisons with later moments in Tudor history. You need to understand what the chief political features of England were in the late fifteenth century.

Why was Henry unlikely to be able to exercise complete control over his new realm? **?**

Recording the strengths and weaknesses of the system of government in a table would give you a clear set of notes. Divide a page up into columns headed 'Strengths' and 'Weaknesses', and use the subheadings in this chapter to group points together. Can you prioritise the points that you make into the greatest strengths and the most serious weaknesses that would have been apparent to Henry VII?

Land and Government

In 1485, there were probably about two million people living in England and Wales. This was considerably less than the number before the bubonic plague epidemic known as the Black Death had swept through the country in 1348–1349. Recovery from such a devastating loss of population was very slow, and was only just beginning at the end of the fifteenth century. Most people lived in the south and east of the country, in rural communities. There were few large towns: London was by far the biggest, with a population of 50 000–70 000. Population centres such as Norwich, Bristol, Exeter, Salisbury and York were much smaller. All shared similar characteristics: they were either ports or main centres of woollen cloth production.

Foreign travellers noticed that people showed a sense of national pride, compared to continental Europeans, who often regarded themselves first and foremost as natives of a region rather than a country. This was probably because, unlike European states, England had been united under one ruler for hundreds of years and national governmental institutions were firmly established. However, in reality, England was more divided than a first glance would reveal. For example, Cornwall was quite distinctive, having its own language, and actually rebelled in 1497. Furthermore, in the more populous South-East, there was a great suspicion of 'the North' and the borderlands with Wales, which were seen as unruly areas. In both regions, some noblemen enjoyed 'franchises' – traditional rights and immunities that limited the authority of the king and government. Durham, for instance, had been ruled as a semi-independent region since the Middle Ages by its prince–bishops. Wales suffered an uneasy relationship with England. It had not been formally united, but the defeat of rebel movements, and a barrage of laws passed in London that restricted the rights of Welshmen, had informally bound the two countries together.

THE CROWN

English kings had wide powers in theory, but were limited in practice by other institutions, and by circumstances such as the uneven nature of central control over the whole land. The king could declare war and make peace, but needed the support of Parliament to grant him the extra taxation needed to fight extended campaigns. He could choose advisers and nominate bishops, but he had to recognise that there were different factions among the nobility and that effective government had broken down in the past when royal favour had not been evenly distributed. He was expected to maintain law and order and to dispense justice, but he did not have a large personal army or numerous civil servants, so he depended heavily on important landowners in the provinces to raise troops and administer his policies. In short, England was ruled by a limited monarchy.

Nonetheless, English kings were not necessarily weak. The title was very much what the person made of it. While people expected 'good lordship' – that the king would govern justly in the interests of his people – he could expect natural obedience from them. Despite the appearance of the Wars of the Roses, it was not in the interests of the nobles constantly to challenge the Crown, and loyalty was as much a feature of their behaviour as personal ambition. The king's authority was established through powerful rituals such as the coronation ceremony, which made him ruler 'by the grace of God' and through symbols such as the coinage, royal crests and palaces. The individual characteristics of the ruler still mattered, as government was built around the person of the king. Henry benefited from being an adult who had been victorious in battle. His determination in plotting to seize the crown showed that he was shrewd and hard-working, and the fact that he was relatively unknown probably also helped.

THE GOVERNMENT

Government was based on the king's court. Here, the king's household not only attended to running the daily life of the court, but also to managing the country. Specialised offices dealt with particular aspects of administration. For example, the king's personal servants in the Chamber had originally dealt with the finances and accounts of his private estates, but had also taken on the responsibility by 1485 of controlling wider government monies. Trusted nobles and churchmen were invited to the King's Council, which organised and regulated the work of the government as well as advising the king on policy matters. Away from the court, Parliament met to pass laws and agree levels and types of taxation. It was not as powerful as today's Parliament, since it met infrequently – when needed by the king – and generally followed the monarch's wishes. During the century before 1485, however, Parliaments had been prepared to defy royal wishes on occasion and had sought to guarantee their privileges, especially the control of taxation. In effect, Parliament could put a brake on the king's plans, but rarely acted in this way.

In the regions, the king's wishes were carried out through an elaborate system of local government that had grown over hundreds of years. Central to it were the Justices of the Peace, usually important landowners, who made sure that laws were enforced, encouraged tax collection, mustered troops and generally supervised the local community. Royal authority depended on the consent and co-operation of a complex network of people, yet what is surprising is how few people were actually involved in managing the country and how few were properly trained officials.

Contemporary views of the land

'The whole country of Britain (which is called England and Scotland) is divided into four parts, England, Scotland, Wales and Cornwall. All these parts are different, either in language or manner of laws. England is the largest and is divided into shires which Englishmen call counties. It is a wealthy land, most fruitful to the south of the Humber, for to the north it abounds in mountains.'
Polydore Vergil

'The riches of England are greater than those of any other country in Europe. This is owing, in the first place, to the great fertility of the soil, which is such that, with the exception of wine, they import nothing from abroad for their subsistence. Next, the sale of their valuable tin brings in a large sum of money to the kingdom; but still more do they derive from their extraordinary abundance of wool which bears such a high price and reputation throughout Europe.'
The Venetian Ambassador, writing in 1497

'England is so fertile that, compared area to area, it surpasses almost all other lands in the abundance of its produce. Its fields, plains, glades and groves abound in vegetation with such richness that they often yield more fruits to their owners than ploughed fields, though these are very fertile in crops and corn. Moreover, pastures are enclosed with ditches and hedges planted over with trees, by which the flocks and herds are protected from the wind and the sun's heat; most of them are irrigated, so that the animals, shut in their pens, do not need watching by day or by night.'
Sir John Fortescue, De Laudibus Legum Angliae, c. 1460

- What general features of the land do these writers praise?
- Think about the factual content and language of the extracts. Which is likely to be the most realistic impression? Why?

THE KEY ISSUES

- How was England linked to the rest of Europe?
- What were the strengths and weaknesses of Henry's new kingdom?

THE KEY SKILLS

Empathy: appreciating the conditions of a different age
Interpretation: deciding on the relevance and usefulness of information
Selection: choosing information to present an argument
Evaluation: reaching an overall judgement

WHAT YOU HAVE TO DO

Having looked at the political structure, you now need to broaden your understanding to include the main social, economic and religious features of the country, as well as the place that England occupied in the wider world.

These broader issues of economic change, religion and culture can be excellent choices as topics for coursework, because they can be narrowed down to how they affected places and people in your local area – or because you could study just one feature of any of them, such as the development of the woollen industry or Cabot's first voyage.

The Renaissance

Literally a 'rebirth' of the arts, the Renaissance flourished in northern Italy in the fifteenth and early sixteenth centuries. Renaissance style was based on a more accurate observation of nature, a stronger belief in the importance of mankind and an attempt to rediscover the classical world of Ancient Greece and Rome. Famous figures of the Renaissance include Leonardo da Vinci and Michelangelo.

England's Place in the World

Although there might have been an emerging sense of national identity, England was not yet a separate and independent nation. Four important strands of life tied the country to continental Europe: trade, traditional alliances and rivalries, the Church and culture.

THE ECONOMY

Agriculture had always provided the main livelihood for people in England. About 90% of the population lived in the countryside. However, the shape and pattern of agriculture were increasingly affected in the fifteenth century by the development of the woollen industry. As G. R. Elton has noted, 'The wealth of England grew less in the fields of wheat and barley than on the backs of sheep.' By Henry's reign, the production of woollen cloth was widely scattered across the country. Wool was the major item of export, often in its raw form to 'finishing' houses in northern Europe. Landowners caught on to this booming trade by turning agricultural land over to sheep farming, even if that meant unpopular enclosure of previously open land and rural unemployment. As a sign of the strengthening of trade, a new class of middlemen had begun to appear, to manage the production and distribution of cloth.

A tailor at work in his home

The picture shows a bolt of cloth being cut and also some of the garments and tools. It was this sort of scene that Henry VII wished to encourage, since exporting raw wool meant that the 'finishing' work and the profits to be made from the production of clothing went abroad

In some regions, other industries had developed. Mining was primitive compared to the mass-producing deep pits of today, but there was a flourishing tin-mining community in Cornwall, which exported most of its ore to Europe, where there was little local tin. Lead was mined in Derbyshire and in valleys in the North and coal was produced in Yorkshire and the North-East.

RELATIONS WITH OTHER COUNTRIES

In the Middle Ages, conflict between England and France had dominated the international scene. The Hundred Years War had been a series of campaigns and skirmishes fought for control of lands in France. It ended disastrously for England in 1453, with the loss of all French lands except Calais, and it revealed that a major transformation in European politics was taking place. Historians talk of the 'rise of the continental monarchies' to describe later fifteenth-century developments, because at the same time that England turned inwards and became divided through the Wars of the Roses, France and Spain were emerging as united countries that were anxious to expand. As they did so, the balance of power shifted southwards, away from the traditional theatre of war in northern France and towards the Mediterranean, where both France and Spain had an interest in the future of the rich but weak Italian states. In the later fifteenth century, England stayed on the sidelines, a useful ally at times to one or other of the new great powers, but not a key player.

THE CHURCH

England in 1485 was staunchly Roman Catholic. People attended church regularly as part of their routine of life, and the Church played an important part in marking out important moments such as births, marriages and deaths. Beyond this, the Church instilled ideas about obedience to authority and the consequences of sinfulness that helped to maintain social stability. As head of the Church, the Pope exercised a spiritual authority over English people by determining how they worshipped and the way in which doctrine was to be understood. In the Middle Ages he had also had the right to appoint senior clergymen, but he had seen this power diminish as English monarchs became more assertive, and less willing to watch an important source of patronage in their kingdom being controlled by someone else. Nonetheless, relations between king and Pope were generally sound. Few would have imagined that a major religious upheaval – the Reformation – would take place within two generations.

CULTURE

More apparent to the well off than the seeds of religious revolution would have been the broader cultural changes that were going on at this time. Caxton's printing press had just been introduced and the first 'mass-produced' books were appearing at the start of Henry VII's reign. On the continent, the intellectual movement known as the Renaissance was beginning to take root, and the new ideas that it created about the arts and learning began to spread into the England at the close of the fifteenth century and in the early sixteenth. Meanwhile, Portuguese navigators had been sailing along the African coast, looking for a sea route to the East. Their voyages began to expand the horizons of European nations far beyond their own continent – as shown by the 1494 Treaty of Tordesillas, which carved up the known world into Portuguese and Spanish spheres of interest.

The Reformation

The Reformation was a religious movement criticising the practices and, from this, the beliefs, of the Roman Catholic Church. Although attacks on the behaviour of priests had been going on throughout the Middle Ages, it was not until Martin Luther, a German monk, openly defied the authority of the Church in 1517 that the Reformation really began. Luther and other reformers created their own churches, shattering the traditional unity of Catholic Europe.

In England, Henry VIII's desperation to rid himself of his first wife, Catherine of Aragon, brought him into conflict with the Pope and led Henry to declare himself Head of the English Catholic Church in 1534. After this, Protestant ideas quickly began to take root, and for much of the later sixteenth and seventeenth centuries there was debate about the precise form that the English Church should take.

John Guy's *Tudor England* (Oxford University Press, 1988) contains a chapter that describes the general condition of the country during the Tudor period. Although it is heavily weighted towards the middle and later sixteenth century, it is a very good starting-point if you want facts and figures about everything from aspects of society to the state of the economy.

THE KEY ISSUES

- How did Henry establish his right to be king?
- Who were his main enemies?

THE KEY SKILLS

Interpretation: deciding on the importance of information
Evaluation: considering the significance of issues
Comparison: identifying similarities and differences

WHAT YOU HAVE TO DO

Now that Henry had won the crown from the Yorkists, there was much to do to ensure that he kept it. You need to identify the ways in which Henry strengthened his position in the first few years of his reign. Looking at some of the later chapters will also help.

In *The Life and Times of Henry VII* (Weidenfeld and Nicolson, 1973), Neville Williams gives a good account of Henry's early life before 1485 and of his first two years in power (see Chapters 1 and 2).

In this chapter, four main threats are referred to: Lovell, Simnel, Warbeck and Suffolk. Use them to organise your thoughts. Once you have researched them thoroughly, you could create a chart to compare them. Possible headings might include Status (what their connection to the crown was), Support (who assisted them and how), Military Threat (whether they invaded, and what happened if they did) and Reaction (how Henry treated them and their supporters).

Securing the Throne

Henry gained the powers and trappings of a king at his coronation on 30 October 1485, but this did not guarantee him people's loyalty or respect. He was an unknown, untried monarch, with a weak claim to the throne, who had relied as much on a surprising victory in battle as on the line of succession. The fates of recent kings did not suggest a long reign: in the generation before Henry seized the crown, kings had been deposed in 1461, 1470, 1471 and 1483.

Henry acted quickly to ensure that his seizure of the crown could be lawfully justified. He declared that his reign had begun on 21 August 1485, the day before the Battle of Bosworth Field. This shrewd tactic enabled him to move against Richard's supporters by claiming that they had acted treasonably. Henry also arranged his coronation ceremony for 30 October, only summoning Parliament when he had been formally crowned king. He restored Lancastrian nobles who had lost land and titles under Richard III, and followed through his promise to marry Elizabeth of York, thus uniting the Lancastrian and Yorkist dynasties. In the spring of 1486, he went on a major journey around his new kingdom to establish his presence in people's minds, and his wife bore him their first child – Arthur – in September 1486. Much later in the reign, Henry was still anxious to make public references to his Lancastrian forefathers. In 1496, for example, he ordered the building of a chapel to house both his tomb and that of Henry VI, and during his reign a more general propaganda effort was mounted to rehabilitate the reputation of that much criticised monarch.

HENRY'S ENEMIES

Henry might have become king, but others had an equal or better claim to that title. Richard III had three nephews who still lived. The ten-year-old Earl of Warwick posed the most troublesome threat, as he was the son of Richard's brother and so carried a claim through the male line. His other nephews were John de la Pole (the Earl of Lincoln) and his younger brother Edmund (later to become the Earl of Suffolk), who were the sons of Richard's sister. They too carried a real claim to the throne, especially since the childless Richard had named the Earl of Lincoln as his successor.

Despite all these possible rivals, Henry had some advantages. He had won the crown through battle and claimed that his victory was the judgement of God. Richard III had been unpopular and been seen as a usurper, someone who had stolen the crown from its rightful owner. For some people, then, Henry's actions in 1485 had corrected a wrongful act. Most importantly, by 1485 the House of York had imploded. Edward IV's family had spent more time after 1471 manipulating events against each other than they had in securing themselves against their enemies, so that after the Battle of Bosworth Field the remnants of the Yorkist dynasty were in complete disarray. In contrast, Henry VII had little close family and, especially, no brothers to compete against.

Elizabeth of York

As the eldest daughter of Edward IV, Elizabeth of York had a claim to the crown in her own right. Like so many royal marriages of the period, Henry's motives were dictated by political considerations, but he was careful not to suggest that he needed his wife's claim to the throne to bolster his own. During his reign, Elizabeth stayed firmly in the background, playing little or no active political role. Her main duty seems to have been to produce healthy sons to continue the Tudor line, and thereby rescue England from future instability and preserve her husband's work. She produced seven children, but only three (Margaret, Henry and Mary) lived to adulthood. Elizabeth died in 1503, having never really recovered from giving birth to Mary

LOVELL'S REBELLION

After the Battle of Bosworth Field, important supporters of Richard III had made themselves scarce. Viscount Lovell and two others had fled to the sanctuary of the Church in Colchester. In early 1486, they reappeared to threaten Henry. Their poor attempts to raise support got nowhere – after all, most people had not been prepared to rally to Richard III's side less than a year before, so it was unlikely that they would suddenly challenge the new king – and Lovell was forced to escape to Flanders. His revolt demonstrated three things: first, that the unsettled times of the later fifteenth century were not yet over; secondly, that there was not much appetite at home for a direct challenge to the king; and, thirdly, that without someone who could offer the people an alternative to Henry, rebellion would be aimless and largely pointless. Future challengers were to take notice of all of these things.

Threats to the crown

How serious were the threats to Henry's crown?

- Henry treated them very seriously. They created a backdrop of dynastic insecurity and uncertainty that persisted throughout his reign. People suspected of plotting with the pretenders or Yorkist claimants were quickly arrested and often executed.
- Conspiracies reached to the heart of the government. Even Henry's closest friends and advisers – such as Sir William Stanley, whose army had swung the fighting at Bosworth Field in Henry's favour – were implicated and arrested.
- Pretenders won support from abroad, particularly from the rulers of Burgundy and the Holy Roman Empire. However, backing was usually short-term and linked to the specific foreign policy aims of these countries. It is doubtful that foreign backers seriously expected Henry to lose the throne.
- The birth of Prince Arthur in 1486, Prince Henry in 1491 and Prince Edmund in 1499 seemed to secure the future of the Tudor dynasty, but the sudden deaths of Edmund and Arthur in 1500 and 1502 revived the uncertainty of the early years of the reign.
- Henry used spies and royal agents to detect threats in their early stages. It has been suggested that some plots were actually engineered by the government to flush out potential traitors.
- The insecurity of his father's reign left a lasting impression on Henry VIII, which may help to explain the lengths he went to during the 1530s and 1540s to ensure a male heir to strengthen the Tudor line.

Simnel, Warbeck and Other Claimants

THE KEY ISSUES

- How serious a threat did 'pretenders' pose?
- How secure was the crown by 1509?

THE KEY SKILLS

Interpretation: deciding on the importance of information
Evaluation: considering the significance of issues
Comparison: identifying similarities and differences

WHAT YOU HAVE TO DO

The problem of dynastic insecurity dogged most of Henry's reign, but was it as real a problem as the king imagined? You need to consider why Henry felt vulnerable as well as the actual threat that rivals posed.

Pretender – an imposter claiming to be heir to the throne; usually set up and backed by powerful groups opposed to the existing ruler, in an attempt to depose them or at least weaken their control

Why did European rulers support pretenders to the English throne?

A detailed account of the career of Perkin Warbeck can be found in Ian Arthurson's *The Perkin Warbeck Conspiracy, 1491–99* (Alan Sutton, 1994). If you are feeling more theatrical, try the Jacobean play *Perkin Warbeck* by John Ford!

Although they might seem strange to modern eyes, pretenders were not uncommon in European politics at this time. There were few reliable pictures of princes. This made it easy for disgruntled family members to swear that the sudden reappearance of someone with a passing, or even no, resemblance to a dead or imprisoned claimant to the throne was the real thing. What was important was the way in which these pretenders could be used to focus pent-up opposition. Although it might be difficult for us to take these threats seriously, Henry VII had no such luxury, since if no credible claimant was prepared to come forward and advance the ambitions of noblemen or foreign rulers, then an incredible one was simply invented for the same dangerous purpose.

LAMBERT SIMNEL

Lambert Simnel was no more than a pawn of the powerful enemies of Henry VII. Even Henry realised this, for when the rebellion was over, he set him to work in the royal kitchens. Simnel was the son of an Oxford tradesman who was set up by his tutor, Richard Symonds, to impersonate the Earl of Warwick. The question of what had happened to the real Earl of Warwick was a matter of public speculation: he had been confined in the Tower of London on the orders of Henry VII, providing an uncomfortable reminder of what had happened when Richard III had seized the throne. Lambert Simnel was supported by the Earl of Lincoln, who probably saw the boy as a means of shaking the crown from Henry's head so that he could pick it up himself. However, it was the support that Simnel received in Ireland, where he was crowned Edward VI, and from Margaret of Burgundy that gave him the military strength to challenge Henry. Simnel's army of Irishmen and German mercenaries landed on the west coast of England in June 1487 and met the king's army at the Battle of Stoke, near Newark in Nottinghamshire. Here, at what some historians describe as the last battle in the Wars of the Roses, Simnel's force was decisively beaten and the troublesome Earl of Lincoln was killed.

PERKIN WARBECK

A second pretender to the throne emerged in even stranger circumstances than the first. Perkin Warbeck appeared in Ireland in 1491 and was acclaimed by local Yorkist nobles as the Duke of York, the younger of the two princes who had supposedly died in the Tower on the orders of Richard III. Warbeck quickly found himself the object of much international attention. More than with Simnel, foreign rulers were prepared to go along with the charade in the hope of getting something out of it. The Scottish king James IV, for instance, was interested in recovering the border town of Berwick, which had been captured in 1482. He hoped that supporting Warbeck would distract Henry from activities on his northern border. When Henry attempted to seize Warbeck in Ireland, he fled to the court of Charles VIII of France. Charles was happy to protect him, as he hoped that this would put pressure on Henry to make a deal over Brittany, a territory that the French king hoped to annex. Once England and France had reached a settlement, Warbeck found that Charles' interest in him had

Perkin Warbeck

evaporated and he was forced to move on to Burgundy. At this time, the Burgundian ruler Maximilian had a strategic interest in the future ownership of northern Italy, which was causing friction with France. Maximilian hoped that, by using the pretender as a bargaining counter, it would force England to help him in the struggle to contain France. For these reasons, Warbeck remained an irritant to Henry for most of the 1490s. Finally, Warbeck foolishly invaded England in July 1495 and was quickly captured. Like Simnel, he was treated leniently because he was only the puppet of more powerful forces, but he abused this by escaping from the king's custody and by allegedly plotting with the imprisoned Earl of Warwick. As punishment, both Warbeck and the earl were hanged in 1499.

LATER CHALLENGES

Although the threat from Warbeck was over, there were other – more real – claimants still alive. Richard III's remaining nephew, Edmund, should have inherited the title of Duke of Suffolk on his father's death. However, Henry's concern about the loyalty and potential threat of this relic of the Yorkist cause led him to force Edmund to accept a 'demotion' to earl. Although Edmund initially accepted this, circumstances changed at the turn of the sixteenth century. Deaths within the royal family made the future of the Tudor line seem much more precarious and raised the importance of the de la Pole bloodline. Recognising, much as Henry had done in 1471, that this sudden advancement put him in real danger, in 1501 Edmund escaped to the court of Maximilian I, from where he provided an uncomfortable reminder that the Yorkist cause was not yet dead. Henry arrested and punished anyone suspected of helping Edmund to flee. It was not until 1506, three years before Henry's death, that this situation was resolved, with the return of the earl.

Who was Perkin Warbeck?

'When the eldest son of Edward, formerly king of England and my dearest lord and father, was miserably put to death and I, then nearly nine years old, was also delivered to a certain lord to be killed, it pleased the Divine Mercy that the lord should preserve me alive and unhurt. First, however, he caused me to swear on the holy sacrament that I would not disclose my name, origin or family to anyone until a number of years had elapsed. Thus I, an orphan, bereaved of my royal father and brother, an exile from my kingdom, and deprived of my country, inheritance and fortune, a fugitive in the midst of extreme perils, led my wretched life in fear and grief and weeping.'

From Perkin Warbeck's letter to Queen Isabella of Castile, seeking Spanish support

'It is first to be known that I was born in the town of Tournai in Flanders and my father's name is John Osbeck. He was controller of the said town, and my mother's name is Katherine de Faro. I put myself in service with a Breton called Pregent Meno, who brought me with him to Ireland. Now when we were arrived in the town of Cork, they of the town (because I was arrayed with cloths and silks of my said master's) came unto me and threatened upon me that I should be the Duke of York, second son to King Edward the fourth.'

From Perkin Warbeck's confession, which he read to the crowd before his execution in 1499

Bearing in mind why Perkin Warbeck wrote each of these documents, can either be trusted totally as evidence of his life? Why is it difficult to be sure of the truth about the careers of pretenders?

THE KEY ISSUE

Why were the nobles seen as a problem?

THE KEY SKILLS

Interpretation: understanding different arguments
Analysis: considering different ideas and reaching conclusions

WHAT YOU HAVE TO DO

There has been much debate about Henry's approach to dealing with his nobility. On the one hand, he undoubtedly exercised greater control over them than his immediate predecessors, but on the other, it might be argued that their threat has been exaggerated anyway. Bear these arguments in mind as you read this chapter.

Summarise the different sorts of roles that nobles played, and then describe why they posed a problem for the king. Think about their Military, Administrative, Legal, Social and Political Importance.

Were the nobles a serious threat?

'The political misfortunes of the last two generations had made them cautious and wary. They, after all, had most to lose by active involvement when high politics led to violence. Events had shown how very small were the forces which could topple a king with disastrous results for those on the losing side.'

J. R. Lander, *The Wars of the Roses* (Alan Sutton, 1992)

The 'Problem of the Nobility'

An unruly nobility had been the central problem in the reigns of each of the last three kings. Henry VII's major domestic policy centred on the need to tame his chief subjects and reduce the threat that they could pose to the stability of his realm. His success was demonstrated by the peaceful succession of Henry VIII in 1509, the first time that a king had reached the throne without the interference of the nobility since 1422. It was achieved, like so much else in the reign, by a combination of effective policies and sheer good fortune.

The Crown's relationship with its chief noblemen was on a sword-edge for much of the fifteenth century. The monarch needed the support and co-operation of the nobility. They provided a vital military function, captaining the royal army and raising troops to aid the king in battle, since he had only a small force of his own. It was expected of noblemen that they should recruit at least some of the men that served under them or, for the more trusted nobles, that they should keep bands of men combat-ready in case of emergencies. As the chief landowners, they were called on to keep law and order in their local communities. At Henry VII's first Parliament in 1485, the king required all those attending to swear oaths to this effect. The nobility also played a significant political role. Medieval ideas of 'good lordship' suggested that the king should consult with leading subjects, and the development of Parliament institutionalised the law-making role of the nobility through the House of Lords. In an age when poor communications isolated the Crown from the people, the nobility played a key role in transmitting and realising the king's wishes. In broader terms, the nobility also moulded cultural changes and offered a constant reminder to the lower orders that society was built as a hierarchy in which everyone had their fixed place.

Without these different forms of co-operation, rulers lacked the money, personnel and might to run the country effectively. Yet this dependence gave nobles opportunities to strengthen and extend their personal power, even at the expense of the king's. In 1399, a group of nobles, angry that Richard II was ignoring their interests and governing badly, rose up and overthrew him, installing Henry, Duke of Lancaster, in his place. During the reign of Henry VI, nobles had exploited the Crown's weakness to carve out stronger local influence, while the 'Wars of the Roses' had shown the destructive effects of an unchecked nobility being exploited by rival contenders for the throne.

HENRY'S AIMS

Henry pursued a careful line, recognising that he was dependent on the nobility and so needed to maintain effective relationships with them, while at the same time containing their ambitions and actions.

He was helped by favourable circumstances. First, the Battle of Bosworth Field had been a decisive victory, since not only was Richard III dead but so were some of the nobles who had fought with him. Few nobles had participated actively in the battle, suggesting that their appetite for an extension of the instability of previous years into the reign of the new king was waning. Secondly, a series of deaths meant that children had become the heads of key families. In the late 1480s, the Earls of Warwick and Northumberland and the Duke of Buckingham were barely in their teens. Thirdly, whereas Edward IV had faced intrigue from his brothers, Henry VII had no close male relatives to oppose him.

Name	Title	Career under Henry VII
Jasper Tudor	Earl of Pembroke, Duke of Bedford	Henry's uncle – he lost his title and lands when he fled into exile in 1471, but was restored to them (and given the additional title Duke of Bedford) in 1485. The dukedom lapsed when he died in 1495
John de la Pole	Earl of Lincoln	Named as heir by Richard III. He supported Lambert Simnel, and was killed at the Battle of Stoke
Edmund de la Pole	Earl of Suffolk	His father had been Duke of Suffolk, but Henry forced Edmund to take a demotion to earl soon after he took the title. As the main Yorkist claimant, he fled to Burgundy in 1501
Richard Neville	Earl of Warwick	A nephew of Richard III. He was imprisoned, aged ten, by Henry VII in 1485. He remained in the Tower until his execution (for alleged support of Warbeck) in 1499
Thomas Howard	Earl of Surrey	He fought against Henry at Bosworth. He was imprisoned until 1489, and some of his lands were seized by attainder. In 1489, he was entrusted with maintaining order in the North after the Yorkshire Rebellion
John de Vere	Earl of Oxford	He supported Henry in exile, and was restored to his lands in 1485. He was fined for illegal retaining in 1504
Henry Percy	Earl of Northumberland	Brought up at court, after his father's death in the Yorkshire Rebellion, he was not allowed to take the title until 1499, when the problem of Warbeck was over. He was placed under recognisance in 1505 for allegedly abducting a royal ward

Prominent noblemen during the reign of Henry VII

The nobility

At the top of the nobility were dukes, originally immediate members of the king's family, but gradually a title extended to a wider circle of people.

Beneath them came earls, viscounts, marquises and barons. Some of these ranks had only been in existence for a comparatively short time.

What marked the nobility out from lesser subjects such as the gentry was their lifestyle and recognition by the monarch, rather than precise measurements such as the extent of their lands or their financial status. In total, there were fewer than 60 individuals who formed the nobility in late fifteenth-century England and this number was reduced further under Henry VII.

What does the information in this table about the fortunes of major noblemen tell us about the different methods that the king used to control them?

Methods of Control

Henry attacked the problem of the nobility from two directions. He sought to limit their numbers by, on the one hand, restricting the creation or advancement of new nobles and, on the other, using legal and financial instruments to curb the actions of existing peers.

TITLES

During Henry's reign, the number of people who could be described as nobles fell by about 25% and those who remained were generally of a lesser status than in previous reigns. Henry used the absence of close family to avoid creating new dukedoms–the only new title that he bestowed was on his uncle, Jasper Tudor, who became Duke of Bedford. He was also reluctant to reward people with lesser noble titles, since this would give them new status, local influence, income and manpower from the lands that they controlled. At the same time, when titles became vacant because there was no direct male descendant, he preferred to absorb them into his personal holdings rather than to create new peers.

ATTAINDERS

Attainders were special laws aimed at specific individuals, to allow the monarch to seize the title and possessions of the accused without trial. They had been used before Henry's reign, but he significantly increased the number, to well over one hundred. There was a flurry of attainders at the start of his reign. By dating his succession back to the day before the Battle of Bosworth Field, Henry was able to declare his enemies traitors and to make an example of nobles sympathetic to the Yorkist cause by stripping them of their lands–signalling to the rest of the nobility that similar fates might befall them. Attainders were not always final, however. Henry reversed those inflicted by Richard III on men who had been loyal to him while he was in exile, and at least one-third of those passed in Henry's reign were later abandoned, although the terms did not always completely restore the fortunes of the nobleman in question. While a severe policy, it was a ruthlessly efficient means of extending the lands of the Crown and decisively weakening potential enemies.

THE COURTS

The threat of legal action in one of the king's courts was another way of restraining the nobility. Henry created new courts within central government to deal with cases involving disobedient nobles. Illegal retaining, breaches of the terms of bonds and recognisances and cases involving general lawlessness were heard by a special group of councillors set up by the Star Chamber Act of 1487. Henry also established the Council Learned in Law, another committee of trusted councillors whose job was to pursue non-payment of fines and dues.

THE KEY ISSUES

- How did Henry try to limit the power and independence of the nobility?
- What effects did his policies have?

THE KEY SKILLS

Interpretation: understanding different arguments
Analysis: considering different ideas and reaching conclusions

WHAT YOU HAVE TO DO

Look at the variety of methods that Henry used to reduce what he believed to be an 'over-mighty' nobility. You should consider not just what he did but what effects his policies had: Did Henry really 'control' the nobility, given his dependence on them for political support? Did his actions help the image of kingship that Henry wished to portray, rather than solve the problem of the nobility's role? Did his policies actually create a deeper gulf between his closest supporters, such as the Duke of Bedford, and other nobles?

Relations with the nobility ...

'The main characteristic of Henry's relations with the nobles is his determination to ensure (through recognisances, fines and other pressures) that they upheld what he himself considered to be the best interests of his kingdom. Henry VII's nobles were expected to co-operate with the king, on the king's own terms.'
Alexander Grant, Henry VII, 1985

To what extent was Henry's success the result of changes in the composition and attitudes of the nobility rather than the effectiveness of his policies?

RETAINING

Henry did not oppose the principle of noblemen keeping personal staffs of paid followers. It was the abuse of this privilege that concerned him, just as it had Edward IV before him. In the king's mind, retaining was associated with lawlessness. By keeping numbers of men in their personal service and by giving them badges or uniforms of office, nobles had what were effectively their own gangs of enforcers. These men could settle disputes much more quickly than the process of the law and could intimidate juries. In return, their master would offer them protection and could exert his own brand of pressure to ensure their 'maintenance'. Henry tried to use the law to attack this problem. Laws were passed in 1487 and 1504 against illegal retaining, repeating and extending similar legislation from Edward IV's reign. The 1504 law in particular was an attempt to introduce new solutions to an old problem. It imposed ridiculously heavy penalties of one hundred shillings per month per person illegally retained by a nobleman. It empowered Justices of the Peace to investigate the problem, set out the process of appeals before the King's court and, most famously, required nobles to seek a special licence to retain, directly from the king. However, there was no real force behind these legislative efforts; after all, it was the very people most likely to be retaining who would have to administer it. Nobles also found other loopholes, such as failing to keep records of wages paid to their staff or re-employing people in different capacities. What made the law at least partly effective was its close connection to the Crown's use of bonds and recognisances.

BONDS AND RECOGNISANCES

Bonds and recognisances were financial contracts that kings used to ensure the continued loyalty of their nobles. Roger Lockyer has called them 'an organised system of coercion', reflecting the fact that they were not primarily ways of raising money, but a means of ensuring obedience. Nonetheless, they yielded £35 000 in 1505, compared to £3000 in 1493. This shows that, while they had been used on occasion early in his reign, continuing the practice of Edward IV, Henry massively increased their use from 1502, when the throne seemed less secure after the death of his eldest son Arthur. At least half of the nobility was put on a bond or recognisance at some point in the reign; and some were placed under more than one, or forced to act as guarantors for other members of their family, or for neighbours, in case of defaults. These financial measures were hated because they were penalties that could be imposed by the king at any time, since there were no clear definitions of what crimes might lead to them. The method of appeals that bypassed ordinary legal processes, and the zealous work of the Council Learned in Law in applying bonds and recognisances, added to their deep unpopularity.

Attainders: a view from below

'The system of attainders involved the transfer of huge quantities of land from old owners to new. These changes brought with them crucial crises of loyalty for the retainers, dependants and tenants of a dispossessed family. In some parts of the country loyalty to a particular family was ingrained and traditional. Any allegiance to a new lord was likely to be brittle and short-lived, especially if the heir of a disinherited family was still alive.'

Charles Ross, *The Wars of the Roses: a Concise History* (Thames and Hudson, 1986)

Bond – a written guarantee which said that if the nobleman failed to meet specific obligations to the king, he would pay a penalty, either a fine or some other forfeit

Maintenance – the support given to retainers by their noble master, usually associated with his interference in local justice to protect them from prosecution

Recognisance – similar to a suspended sentence; a nobleman would agree to be of good behaviour in future or would pay a fine or some other forfeit

Retaining – the common practice of keeping men as personal servants of a nobleman

---

In the Routledge 'Lancaster Pamphlet' *Henry VII: the Importance of his Reign in English History* (1985), Alexander Grant gives an excellent summary of how historians' views about the relationship between Crown and nobility have changed.

THE KEY ISSUE

What were the principal sources of royal income?

THE KEY SKILLS

Comprehension: understanding the main features of a topic
Interpretation: deciding on the usefulness of information

WHAT YOU HAVE TO DO

Sometimes, examination questions just focus on this aspect of Henry's reign, reflecting the importance that is traditionally attached to the subject of finances. Understanding the sources of income can be a useful starting-point for essays. You could organise an answer around the different types of ordinary and extraordinary income, explaining what happened to each. Make sure that your notes are clear on the wide range of available sources of income and look at more detailed texts for further essays on them.

Devise a pattern diagram to record the different sources of Crown income. As a starting-point, space the words 'Ordinary' and 'Extraordinary' well apart on a fresh sheet of paper and add in the different types of each income around these headings. Any that might seem to have elements of each sort of income could be attached to both headings if you think about layout carefully.

1 Using the information in this chapter, can you prioritise the different types of income, either by the amount that they yielded or the importance that Henry attached to them?
2 How did Henry's methods of raising money change as his reign developed?

Sources of Income

Reform of the financial system had begun under Edward IV, but the effects of these changes only reached their fullest potential under Henry VII. While Henry's reputation rests squarely on his revival of Crown finances, interpretations of his behaviour have been pushed to extremes by those who believe he was a miser, obsessed with making money. More realistically, it is fair to say that he understood the need for a solid financial base and was determined to exploit fully all opportunities to gain income. By the end of his reign, he had put finances back on a firm footing, but there were limitations, both in the extent of his success compared to other European rulers and in the reaction of his subjects to his efforts.

It was relatively unusual for rulers to tax their subjects directly. Instead, kings derived income from a wide range of traditional sources. Historians usually divide these into two broad types: 'ordinary' revenues (sometimes called 'customary' or 'prerogative') and 'extraordinary' revenues. Although there is no hard and fast distinction between them, ordinary income was generally any revenue that the king had a personal right to collect or which had been permanently granted to him. According to medieval theory, the king was obliged to use this sort of income to maintain the kingdom, to pay for the running of government and to keep his household. Extraordinary revenue was generally anything that had to be specially granted by Parliament or some other body. It was not automatic income in the way in which ordinary revenues were, but was usually granted to meet particular needs, such as foreign wars, that the king would be unable to afford from his own resources.

ORDINARY REVENUE

By the end of Henry's reign, nearly half of his income came from his royal estates. Unlike Edward IV, Henry rarely gave away lands to his supporters, so as he seized new estates – through Acts of Attainder, escheats and one-to-one agreements with noblemen – he became not only the chief landowner in England, but also the largest single landowner for over five hundred years.

As king, Henry could also turn to an impressive array of feudal rights to help raise money. Medieval feudalism placed the monarch in the position of owner of all the lands in the realm, which he distributed to his nobles in return for their loyalty and service. As their overlord, the king could demand a payment whenever changes took place in landholding arrangements. While much of the feudal system had withered away by Henry's reign, this financial relationship had not. If a landowner died before his son had reached maturity, Henry could claim 'wardship', which effectively made him guardian of the boy and his estates. When a ward came of age, Henry could then demand 'livery', a payment to allow the transfer of the estate to its new owner. If heirs or heiresses wished to marry, the king could expect further payments. Even if lands transferred smoothly from father to son, there was still a charge called a 'relief'.

As head of the legal system, the king was also entitled to money raised from fines or other financial penalties imposed on convicted criminals. The increased use of bonds and recognisances during his reign boosted this sort of income significantly. Henry also benefited from the receipts from tonnage (an import tax) and poundage (an export duty). Both were granted to the king for life by Parliament at the start of the reign – and could yield impressive amounts when the economy flourished, as it began to during his reign.

EXTRAORDINARY REVENUE

By the fifteenth century, Parliament had become established as the main source of additional funding for major projects such as wars. However, this role had, on occasion, given Parliament an unwelcome opportunity to interfere in royal finances by demanding to scrutinise the account books or debate how the money was being spent. So, while Henry VII had to resort to parliamentary grants at various times in his reign, he preferred to avoid making these requests in case strings were attached. In agreeing to a grant, Parliament was effectively authorising a one-off direct tax on the king's subjects. This traditionally took the form of 'Fifteenths' and 'Tenths', which were types of property tax, levied in rural and urban areas respectively. Henry tried to find alternatives to this unpopular form of taxation, including a primitive form of income tax, but with limited success.

Other than parliamentary grants, Henry could also turn to loans and benevolences from his leading subjects to raise money in an emergency. Whereas loans were generally repaid, benevolences were not, and so ranked alongside bonds and recognisances as an unpopular way of extorting money from the rich.

Finally, the Church also made infrequent contributions to royal finances, usually to help finance wars against the enemies of the Pope. Although the king was not yet head of the English Church, he did have the right to nominate people to vacant bishoprics. This offered opportunities both to sell these jobs to the highest bidder or deliberately to leave them unfilled so that the Crown could take income from the lands held by that bishop.

THE RANGE OF ROYAL FINANCES

So, Henry could draw upon a wide range of sources for finances; some personal, others not. He could exploit the economy, the Church, the law, his nobility and his lands for income. Henry's revenues came from a combination of all of the following:

- rents from royal estates
- income from newly acquired lands
- feudal dues such as wardship, livery and relief
- fines imposed by his courts
- bonds and recognisances
- receipts from import and export taxes
- parliamentary grants of taxation
- loans from his nobles
- opportunities to raise money from the Church

The foundations of Henry's success

Henry's reputation as a shrewd financial manager rests on a number of achievements:

- his cunning, and at times ruthless, exploitation of existing sources of revenue rather than an innovative approach
- his meticulous personal interest in financial matters and his focused approach to raising revenue once he had settled in as king
- his strengthening of the existing machinery for managing royal finances
- his careful approach to spending – while he recognised the need for a suitably lavish court, he was reluctant to waste money on expensive foreign wars or on rewarding followers

Benevolences – gifts of money to the Crown that were unlikely to be repaid

Escheat – the right of the king to take land back into Crown ownership if there was no successor to the deceased landowner

Feudalism – a social and economic structure that grew in the eleventh century, which organised rank in society on the basis of landholding and provided for a complex system of duties and obligations between people on different levels of the social scale; it had deteriorated by the fifteenth century, perhaps into 'bastard feudalism', which could most obviously be seen in the practice by major landowners of retaining

Livery – the badges or uniforms worn by a nobleman's retainers

Wardship – control of the estates of a family, by the Crown or a nominated person, while the title-holder was still a child

How Revenue was Managed

THE KEY ISSUES

- How was the collection and distribution of royal finances organised?
- How effective were Henry's financial policies?

THE KEY SKILLS

Analysis: judging information
Comparison: identifying similarities and differences

WHAT YOU HAVE TO DO

All writers agree that Henry was effective at raising money, but it is possible to detect different degrees of approval. Was Henry 'ruthless', 'obsessed with making money' or simply 'efficient'? Be sure that you do not just uncritically accept his achievements: consider the limitations of his policies as well.

The Cornish Rebellion

This was the most serious popular disturbance of Henry VII's reign. His attempts to raise money to defend against a possible invasion from Perkin Warbeck through Scotland drew much opposition in Cornwall. Arguing that taxes were too high and the use of them too remote for Cornish interests, at least 10 000 rebels marched towards London to present their grievances to the king. Henry took their actions seriously. He broke off preparations to strike against Scotland and mustered an army of about 25 000 men to defend London. The rebels were ill-prepared to fight and were quickly crushed. Their leaders were executed in public and heavy fines imposed on anyone suspected of having been involved.

The Exchequer was the traditional office that dealt with financial matters. It had developed in the twelfth century and was responsible for receiving money from a network of collectors across the country, for storing this income and for making payments on demand to officials and creditors of the Crown. It also audited the account books, ensuring that they were accurate and that the Crown was receiving its proper share of any income. However, the Exchequer was not part of the royal household, but a separate specialised department of government. This made it difficult for kings to have complete control over what it was doing. Moreover, as the administration of finances became more complex in the fifteenth century, the Exchequer became a slow and clumsy way of handling finances. It was not uncommon for financial short-cuts to be developed (such as allowing tax collectors to pay creditors directly rather than sending money to the Exchequer, or keeping separate accounts of the finances of estates such as the royal Duchy of Lancaster), which sidelined and weakened its control.

THE DEVELOPMENT OF THE CHAMBER

Edward IV had recognised the shortcomings of the Exchequer and had transferred some of its functions to the Chamber, an office in his royal household. This was better for the monarch: it allowed him to monitor closely income and expenditure through the account books, to decide on the order in which creditors would be paid and, most importantly, it gave the king direct control over money coming in, which could be vital in an emergency. Henry VII also recognised the value of Chamber finance and diverted upwards of 90% of revenue management to it by the end of his reign, but in the 1480s his inexperience, his more pressing interests in securing the crown and the general dilapidation of royal finances meant that the Exchequer briefly resumed control.

Henry used the system already developed by Edward IV, but that did not mean that he merely accepted it. Henry's achievement was to strengthen and extend aspects of the Yorkist financial management system to maximise its efficiency and his income:

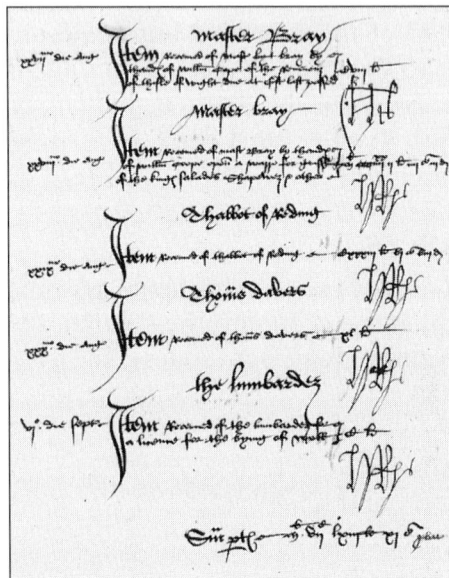

A page from a receipts book from the reign of Henry VII, showing the king's signature against the entries

- he played a strong personal role in managing his income – he regularly checked and signed receipts, even for trivial amounts, and interviewed collectors about their work
- he strengthened the personnel in the Chamber by using what Richard Britnell calls 'professional careerists' and men of proven loyalty to the king, such as Sir Reginald Bray, Sir Thomas Lovell (who was Treasurer to the Chamber until 1492) and Sir Thomas Heron (Treasurer from 1492)
- because the Chamber did not have the auditing machinery of the Exchequer, Henry appointed 'surveyors' to check the receipts from different sources on income – for example, Sir John Hussey was Surveyor of the King's Wards from 1503
- he also recognised that the Chamber lacked the judicial machinery to pursue and prosecute debtors, and so gave the Council Learned in Law the responsibility of acting as a court of law to settle disputes and to collect debts

THE REACTION TO HENRY'S POLICIES

Henry exploited his sources of income to their fullest, especially after 1502 when Prince Arthur died and the future of the Tudor dynasty again looked shaky. Individual nobles were undoubtedly inconvenienced and angered by the more intrusive aspects of the king's policies, such as forced loans, bonds and recognisances, but few actively resisted paying. There was, however, general hostility to the actions of Dudley and Empson in the Council Learned in Law, as they enthusiastically rooted out debtors. Neither man survived Henry VII by very long and this aspect of financial management was quickly shelved by Henry VIII.

Ordinary people also reacted to Henry's financial demands. On two occasions the taxation arising from parliamentary grants caused significant popular rebellions. In 1489, it was agreed that the Brittany campaign should be funded by a grant of £100000. Attempts to collect taxes to meet this sum were resisted in Yorkshire, which was already suffering from poor harvests. It was in the course of this rebellion that the Earl of Northumberland was killed. In 1497, a new grant to fund an expedition in the north against Perkin Warbeck and James IV of Scotland was rejected in Cornwall, where people simply refused to pay for such a distant project. Both rebellions were suppressed, but at a time of dynastic insecurity and Yorkist pretenders, they were serious enough to cause alarm.

THE ROYAL FINANCES BY 1509

No one is absolutely certain how wealthy the Crown was at the time of Henry's death, but some facts can be agreed upon: the Crown had enough money to meet its debts and there was a surplus of cash left in the treasury for Henry VIII. The total annual income of the Crown was probably in the region of £110000–133000. The principal revenues contributing to this figure were the incomes from royal estates and feudal dues (estimated at £42000) and customs duties (about £40000).

The limitations of Henry's achievement

'Recognition of Henry VII's undoubted and major achievement in restoring royal finances must not obscure the fundamental truth that by European standards the English monarchy was under-endowed, circumscribed in its freedom of action, and dependent upon a considerable degree of co-operation, however grudgingly given, from those who were subject to it.'
Alexander Grant, Henry VII, 1985

'The sophistication of Henry's financial system must not be exaggerated. The Chamber's accounting system was crude – with all expenditure recorded in one lump sum – and there was no means of enforcing payment ... There were no innovations and no new sources of revenue were discovered. He merely continued Edward IV's policy of more effective exploitation of the royal estates.'
John Lotherington (editor), The Tudor Years, 1994

How did Henry's methods of raising money help his other aims?

In the Hodder and Stoughton 'Access to History' book, *Henry VII* (1991), Caroline Rogers gives a very detailed summary of all the different sources of income that Henry could exploit.

What does the receipts book tell us about Henry's view of his role as king?

Central Government

In 1485, Henry was faced with the major task of quickly stamping his authority on the country that he had just won by force of arms. Effective government was critical for many reasons: it raised the prestige of the king, subdued the ambitions of the nobility, allowed efficient generation of revenues and promoted law and order among the king's subjects. The circumstances of his succession made Henry reluctant to innovate. He had no personal experience or training in government and knew that major upheavals in personnel early in the reign would breed discontentment and inefficiency. So, much of the structure and many of the people who had worked for the Yorkist kings survived the arrival of the Tudor dynasty.

THE KING AND HIS HOUSEHOLD

Fifteenth-century government was conducted on a much smaller scale than its modern counterpart. At its heart was the person of the king and the court that revolved around him. Henry was a more active monarch than his immediate predecessors, or his son. He consulted regularly and widely before taking action, closely scrutinised royal finances and took all major decisions personally. He was both king and chief minister in an age of centralised personal government.

Within the household, the Royal Council was the hub of government activity. In it sat the king's most trusted followers – noblemen, clergymen and lesser-ranking friends. They met as and when the king needed to discuss major policies such as defence or taxation plans, and to offer advice. They also had an important legal function, acting as a court of justice in particular cases. Henry made no dramatic changes to the composition of the Council, using the same number of men of a similar rank to those who had served his predecessors. However, he did supplement its work with some more specialised courts, such as the Court of Audit, the Court of Requests (which revived Richard III's scheme of offering cheap access to justice for the poor) and, most notoriously, the Council Learned in Law. With this increased specialisation came a greater expertise among administrators, especially as Henry tended to keep loyal men in the same jobs for a long time.

Elsewhere in the household, as we have seen, the management of royal finances shifted decisively towards the Chamber. Another development which has been debated by historians was the strengthening of the Privy Chamber. It has been suggested that, in the 1490s, Henry's fears of treason by supporters of Perkin Warbeck, and more general concerns that some of his trusted advisers were becoming too powerful, led him to shift the heart of government business into his Privy Chamber. This was a room to which few people had right of access, since the king conducted his most personal affairs

---

THE KEY ISSUES

- How was the king's household organised?
- How did the work of the household develop during Henry's reign?
- What role did Parliament play in royal government?

THE KEY SKILLS

Investigation: researching an issue
Interpretation: drawing conclusions
Comparison: identifying similarities and differences

WHAT YOU HAVE TO DO

Without good government, Henry could not be an effective king, so this aspect of the topic is crucial to understanding his success. Make sure that you are really clear about how government was organised (reading Chapters 4 and 5 alongside this one will help), since this will also allow you to judge the alterations and additions made by later Tudor rulers. As always, ask our basic questions about what Henry did – about his aims, methods, success and impact.

Research the names, jobs and importance of some of Henry's advisers. Were they an important part of government? **?**

Meetings of Parliament in Henry's reign

1 November 1485–March 1486
2 November–December 1487
3 January 1489–February 1490
4 October 1491–March 1492
5 October–December 1495
6 January–March 1497
7 January–April 1504

there, such as washing and dressing. There, the king could be removed from the general intrigues of the court and could concentrate on the business of state with few unwanted interruptions.

THE LEGAL SYSTEM

For centuries, the king had been recognised as the 'fount of law', since he appointed judges and, through them, determined what was legal and what was not. Within central government there were several specialised courts, such as the Admiralty Court, which dealt with maritime cases, and the more general courts of King's Bench and Common Pleas, which heard a range of civil and criminal cases. Through these courts, the king was able to send judges around the country, hearing cases that could not be decided by his Justices of the Peace in local hearings. Henry wanted the legal system to work effectively because it was an important way of ensuring that his power was accepted and because the fines imposed by the courts added to his treasury. During his reign, attempts were made to improve the quality and efficiency of justice. Legislation was passed to prevent the selection of biased juries, new courts were established, such as the Council Learned in Law, and the Court of Chancery continued to develop as a quicker alternative to the more complex proceedings of the courts of King's Bench and Common Pleas. These changes, coupled with the growth of a more professional staff of trained lawyers, helped to create a well-respected and effective legal system by 1509.

PARLIAMENT

The role of Parliament was not to govern the country directly by making policy decisions, but to pass the necessary laws that would allow the king's policies to be realised. Fourteenth- and early fifteenth-century Parliaments had occasionally criticised these policies and tried to strengthen their own privileges to help them fight against what they considered to be bad government but, in the main, Parliament worked co-operatively with the monarch.

Henry did not make extensive use of Parliament. He only called it seven times during his reign, mostly in the first decade when frosty relations with France, problems with pretenders and the search for security drove him to seek legislative backing and more money. The most important function of Parliament each time Henry called it was its customary job of voting taxation. Its law-making role was secondary, and its value as a mouthpiece for the Commons and Lords to express views about policy came a poor third. Occasionally – when he needed to win the widest support for a major initiative – Henry resorted to the medieval practice of summoning a Great Council that consisted of just the House of Lords rather than a full Parliament but, again, this was rare. Henry preferred to keep Parliament at arms length as much as possible.

John Morton

Of all the people who worked for Henry VII, John Morton perhaps has the best claim to being the king's closest colleague and chief minister. Morton had supported Edward IV in the 1470s and had been appointed Bishop of Ely in 1479, but had turned against the Yorkist cause when Richard III had become king. His activities between 1483 and 1485 marked him out as a true friend of the future king: he warned Henry of Richard's attempt to extradite him from Brittany in 1485, allowing Henry to escape to France, and he was active before this in canvassing support for the Tudor cause among discontented Yorkists.

Once Henry became king, he rewarded Morton with the post of Lord Chancellor, the Crown's main legal officer and principal manager of royal business. Morton also moved upwards from the bishopric of Ely to become Archbishop of Canterbury in 1486. He was considered a shrewd and efficient servant of the king, and seems to have been a close friend and adviser of Henry, despite a significant age difference.

The story of 'Morton's Fork' illustrates these characteristics: in pursuit of loans for the king, Morton is said to have presented people with a catch-22. If they were obviously wealthy because of their dress and behaviour, he pressed them for money on the grounds that they could easily afford it. If people seemed less well off, he suggested that this was because they must have put plenty into savings, and so still squeezed the loan from them!

Review Chapters 4, 5, 7 and 8 to find examples of types of legislation passed by Parliament under Henry VII.

THE KEY ISSUES

- What problems did regional and local government pose for the Crown?
- How did Henry tackle these problems?
- Was his kingdom well-governed?

THE KEY SKILLS

Investigation: researching an issue
Interpretation: drawing conclusions
Comparison: identifying similarities and differences

WHAT YOU HAVE TO DO

Always remember that 'government' does not just consist of those close to the centre of national power. Feudalism, poor communications and the conflicts of the fifteenth century meant that much of the real power was exercised locally. The king could issue orders, but needed willing people across England to implement them. Use these pages to determine the extent to which Henry developed sub-central government.

- Using the whole of this chapter, draw a diagram to represent the structure of government in Henry's reign, using different colours for the traditional and new parts of it.
- The issues of continuity and change in government can be neatly summarised in a table. Use these headings and put in comments about personnel, existing and new institutions, and the relative importance of different institutions. Don't worry if you think that there are both continuities and changes in the same areas – it is exactly this sort of complex understanding that examiners like!

Regional and Local Government

Henry had a smaller immediate family than Edward or the earlier Lancastrian kings, so he was unable to use them in government in the same way. Although Arthur and Henry were given various responsibilities (such as heading the Council of Wales or acting as Lord Lieutenant in Ireland), these were purely honorary, since both were too young to understand or manage important duties. However, Henry was also determined not to make the same mistake as Edward IV and create nobles with strong regional power bases. Because of this, his policies towards regional government were inconsistent and pragmatic, responding to the situation in each area.

WALES AND THE NORTH

Edward IV had created the Council of Wales and the Marches, but Richard III had abandoned it in 1483. Henry had good reason to be grateful to Wales: it was his homeland and had been the launchpad for his invasion of England in 1485. Henry restored the Council and followed a policy of appointing Welshmen to it. It flourished and was to be further strengthened by Henry's successors, who continued to develop it into an effective system of regional government.

Henry had much less reason to view northern England with favour. It was far from the guiding influence of his government, more lawless, more Yorkist and more rebellious than the rest of the country. Richard III had created the Council of the North, but some writers claim that Henry chose to allow it to lapse. Instead, he used the opportunity created by the murder of the Earl of Northumberland in the Yorkshire Rebellion of 1489 to install the Earl of Suffolk to replace him, even though Suffolk had no lands in the North, nor local experience. What mattered to Henry was that Suffolk had the social clout necessary to maintain order, but not the power base to threaten the Crown. Henry was also helped by other circumstances: whatever hatreds northerners had of him, they were not anxious to see Scottish armies sweep into their land and so were less inclined to pose problems for Henry during the troubled 1490s.

IRELAND

Henry was supposedly Lord of Ireland, but this had little meaning in much of the country outside Dublin, where real power lay with traditional family clans. Henry was interested in Ireland only because it sympathised with the Yorkists and was the starting-point for the careers of Simnel and Warbeck. At the beginning and end of his reign, Henry continued the tradition of relying on local nobles effectively to rule on his behalf. However, when the Earl of Kildare, Henry's Lord Deputy, showed reluctance to act against Perkin Warbeck, Henry tried a second approach based on direct rule. He sacked Kildare, appointed Englishmen to senior positions in Irish government and asked the new Lord Deputy, Sir Edward Poynings, to implement reforms that would tie Ireland more closely to the English Crown. Poynings' Law of 1494 tried to do this by undermining the independence of the Irish Parliament. Views about the success of these moves differ: Henry abandoned direct rule, probably because of the cost, and reinstated the Earl of Kildare and traditional forms of government in 1496 – but after this there were no major difficulties from Ireland, so perhaps the reminder of what the king could do was enough to subdue problems.

A sixteenth-century map of Ireland

LOCAL GOVERNMENT

Effective government depended on the co-operation of a network of people at a regional and local level to implement the king's wishes. Henry continued to rely on the nobles in the regions but, at a more local level, the responsibilities of the Justice of the Peace had been increasing for many years, partly at the expense of noblemen, and Henry continued and speeded up this practice. JPs were unpaid officials, usually members of the gentry, a well-to-do class below the nobility, and sometimes professionally trained lawyers. They were empowered to administer the local community in a variety of ways, such as making tax assessments, checking weights and measures, and regulating licensed premises such as ale-houses. They also had an important legal role as well: they were expected to enforce the king's laws, review the composition of juries and generally to ensure that suspects were brought to justice. During Henry's reign there was a stream of legislation that extended and strengthened these administrative and legal duties, which has led the historian John Guy to suggest that 'there was a perceptible shift before the Reformation towards the idea of a Crown-controlled magistracy'.

Detailed descriptions of the system of government can be found in all of the books on Henry VII. You should find Chapters 5–7 of *Henry VII* by Roger Lockyer and Andrew Thrush (Longman Seminar Studies in History, 3rd edn, 1997) particularly useful. Each of these chapters deals with a different aspect of government: institutions at the centre, regional government and Parliament.

Key features of government

In the late fifteenth century the key features were as follows:
- the hands-on role played by the monarch and his courtiers in the royal household
- the small range of central government activities, most obvious the economy, dealing with other countries and overseeing justice
- the limited number of officials working in government, and the reliance on wealthy families
- the blurring of boundaries between administration (carrying out government decisions) and justice (enforcing those decisions)
- in local government, the crucial role played by local officials and by nobles with land interests in the region

The Domestic Economy

England had been undergoing a slow economic transformation for over a century before Henry became king. The Black Death of 1348–1349 had been a catastrophe, killing as much as one-third of the population. The temporary economic bargaining power that it gave to the survivors to negotiate rents without personal service had contributed to the breakdown of the feudal system and to the first mass peasant uprising – the Peasant's Revolt of 1381. Rural depopulation and the attraction of large profits had lured some landowners away from producing crops and into sheep farming, shattering customary patterns of work and even the appearance of the countryside. All of this had also triggered social change. The boundary between the nobility and the gentry was becoming blurred as fortunes were built from the woollen industry by people of lower social status, while some of those at the bottom of the social scale were increasingly in danger of falling into long-term unemployment and poverty.

AGRICULTURE

In many ways, Henry's reign merely continued these trends. The enclosing of lands continued and was a source of continuing protest by those who were adversely affected. Parliament passed various laws, such as anti-enclosure legislation, and an Act of 1489 required land over 20 acres that had been farmed as agricultural land for three years to be maintained as such, but these efforts tended to be half-hearted, lamenting what was going on but failing to offer really workable solutions. Henry was caught between the need to tackle immediate social problems that were causing unrest and his desire not to offend the landowners, whose support he desperately needed to govern effectively and whose revenues from the woollen trade were swelling his treasury. So, rural communities continued to be affected by engrossing (the creation of larger farms by merging smallholdings), depopulation, unemployment and its attendant problems. However, it is possible to exaggerate the extent of the change that was taking place. Caroline Rogers warns us against taking too pessimistic a view. She points out that very little land was actually enclosed at this time and that most of it was done with the agreement of all concerned.

WOOL

The woollen industry continued to strengthen its grip on the economy. It was overwhelmingly the biggest sector of the export market, accounting for about 90% of all goods leaving English shores in this period. The interest shown by the government in the woollen industry was hardly surprising: Henry benefited directly from its success because one source of his ordinary revenue was customs duty. By the end of his reign, income from taxes on imports and exports had doubled to £40 000 per year.

THE KEY ISSUE

What were the strengths and weaknesses of England's economy?

THE KEY SKILLS

Investigation: identifying a range of ideas

Evaluation: reaching conclusions

Comparison: recognising continuity and change

WHAT YOU HAVE TO DO

Make sure that your notes reflect the central importance of wool to the economy and the tensions that this produced in land use. Be careful not to assume that Henry had a strong or well-developed interest in the economy. Much decision-making lay with individual landowners.

The economic effects of the Wars of the Roses

The traditional view of the conflict between the Lancastrians and Yorkists as a destructive struggle that devastated the country has long been discredited. Charles Ross, in *The Wars of the Roses*, is at pains to underplay their effects:

'English life and civilisation in general were remarkably little affected by thirty years of sporadic conflict. There was very little material devastation, little pillage or plundering. No major towns were looted or pillaged, or even systematically besieged.'

However, not all writers feel that their effects should be discounted. D. M. Loades, in *Politics and the Nation 1450–1660*, says that: 'All this is true, but it should not cause us to ignore the innumerable trespasses and assaults, the petty sieges and savage little affrays. The fact that England did not resemble a country devastated by an invading army does not mean that the effects of the troubles were trivial, or localised in their incidence.'

Men at work in an orchard
This picture shows one of the variety of agricultural practices that had developed by the late fifteenth century, and is probably taken from a book of husbandry (a manual describing techniques of production and management)

The Crown adopted a protectionist approach. Henry's Parliaments legislated to restrict the flow of raw wool out of the country, because this was preventing the development of a large-scale finishing industry in England and leaving buyers of cloth dependent on expensive imports from the continent. Amongst the measures adopted were laws giving priority to domestic buyers over foreign merchants when raw wool came on the market and heavy taxes on traders attempting to export the raw material. The success of Henry's policies can be seen by the 60% rise in exports of finished cloth by the end of his reign and the 30% fall in exports of raw wool.

OTHER DEVELOPMENTS

Commerce needed ships. Too much trade for Henry's liking was carried into and out of English ports by foreign crews. Navigation Acts were passed in 1485 and 1489 to force English merchants to use their own country's ships in preference to foreign ones. Henry also offered tax incentives to encourage people to build merchant ships.

Despite all these changes, and more, such as the standardisation of weights and measures in 1497 and the introduction of new coins, there were weaknesses in the economy. The principal long-term problem was the imbalance caused by the strength of the woollen trade. It was simply too easy to rely on the profits of this industry and ignore the proper development of other sectors. Compared to its neighbours, England lagged well behind in the range of goods under large-scale production and had an unhealthy dependence on imports.

What does this picture tell us about fifteenth-century agriculture? Think about land use, products, tools and techniques, and gender roles.

Neville Williams looks at the development of 'Town and Country' in Chapter 6 of *The Life and Times of Henry VII* (Weidenfeld and Nicolson, 1973).

Tudor coins

As king, Henry VII was responsible for the coinage of the realm. This meant that he could order changes in their value, style and the amount in circulation. For the first time in 100 years, Henry used these powers to order a wholesale change in English coinage. There were 11 basic coins in circulation, ranging from the golden sovereign through the ryal, worth half the value of a gold sovereign, and the gold angel, worth approximately one-third of the value of a sovereign, to the silver groat and the penny, half-penny and farthing. No official paper money existed in England until the formation of the Bank of England in 1694, even though it was much more portable than bags of cash. Henry also changed the appearance of the coins by insisting on a portrait of the crowned king on one side of the higher denominations. However, problems remained: people were reluctant to accept these new coins at first and many foreign coins were still in circulation (because the value of the metal that they were made from mattered more than where they came from).

THE KEY ISSUE

How successfully did Henry promote England's trade with other countries?

THE KEY SKILLS

Investigation: identifying a range of ideas

Evaluation: reaching conclusions

Comparison: recognising continuity and change

WHAT YOU HAVE TO DO

It is important to make a judgement about Henry's priorities when dealing with other countries, and this chapter and the next should help you to do that. Which was more important: the security of the crown on his head, or the money and reputation he gained from trade? Also, keep in mind the other basic themes – methods, success and effects.

Use the headings Agriculture, Wool, Other Industries, Overseas Trade (which can be divided into Burgundy, Spain, northern Europe and the Mediterranean) and Exploration.

The Treaty of Medina del Campo

- Customs duties between England and Spain were to be reduced to make trade easier.
- Discussions would take place regarding a marriage alliance between Prince Arthur and Princess Catherine of Aragon.
- Neither side would assist anyone rebelling against the other.
- Both sides would work together to defend their lands and would not make agreements with France without consulting each other first.

Trading Partners and Rivals

Henry was keen to promote commerce, not least because it brought him income from customs and excise duties, but it was not his first priority. It can be difficult to disentangle England's trade dealings with other countries from the king's diplomatic manoeuvrings, because Henry was prepared to use commercial relations as a branch of foreign policy and to compromise or even abandon trading enterprises when they brought him into conflict with other countries and threatened the security of the Tudor dynasty.

TRADE AGREEMENTS

An important part of the Crown's commercial policy was the negotiation of trade agreements with other states. These agreements regulated the terms of trade and dealt with matters such as tariffs and the carriage of goods. Henry's outstanding achievement lay in forging favourable trade terms with Spain and Burgundy, and in injecting political bonuses for himself into these agreements. England had a long-standing friendship with Portugal, but the unification of Spain opened up possibilities elsewhere in the Iberian peninsula. In 1489, Henry negotiated the Treaty of Medina del Campo, an action described by Caroline Rogers as 'the most significant achievement of his foreign policy'. It obliged both countries to reduce customs duties on each other's goods and had the additional benefit of compelling Spain not to support Henry's enemies. After the disagreements of the early 1490s, Henry also won favourable trade terms with Burgundy in the 'Magnus Intercursus' of 1496. This restored the rights of English merchants in Antwerp and went on to allow them to trade freely and without paying duties in most of the Burgundian lands. Henry also attempted to exploit Philip of Burgundy's desire to become King of Castile after the death of Queen Isabella, by persuading him to agree to the so-called 'Malus Intercursus' in 1506. This treaty would have significantly strengthened the already favourable trading privileges of English merchants, but was quickly abandoned in the face of stiff opposition from Burgundian traders and further changes in the international balance of power.

THE WOOL TRADE

Henry also attempted to strengthen access to foreign markets for English finished cloths. He enjoyed mixed success, partly because he was too quick to use wool as a weapon in his efforts to defeat pretenders. Most cloth was sent to the port of Antwerp for re-sale and distribution in Europe. This made trade relations with Burgundy extremely important, but the willingness of its rulers to support Simnel and Warbeck caused an exasperated Henry to put an embargo on trade in 1493 and attempt to develop the English enclave of Calais as an alternative outlet. While the collapse of links with Antwerp had potentially disastrous effects for English merchants, the Calais project never really took off. It was fortunate that the resolution of differences with Burgundy in the late 1490s soon restored the primacy of Antwerp. In the Mediterranean, Henry was also prepared to use the wool trade as a lever to gain advantage. He recognised the dominance of Venice in regional trade, and so he offered a monopoly of the sale of English cloths to Florence in 1490 as a counterbalance. Again, this ultimately worked in England's favour by forcing Venice to relax strict trade rules, but this had as much to do with the outbreak of the Italian Wars in 1494 as with Henry's seemingly reckless gambling with the lucrative wool trade.

THE HANSEATIC LEAGUE

Henry's manoeuvrings were generally successful, if bumpy at times, in protecting English trade with France, Spain and Burgundy, and he was also able to make some inroads into the Mediterranean by driving a wedge between Florence and Venice. However, the great disappointment with regard to his commercial efforts was in northern Europe. English merchants were keenly interested in expanding trade with the states that bordered the Baltic Sea. Henry had some success in negotiating fishing agreements and general commercial links with Denmark and Norway, but found the north German towns that formed the Hanseatic League unwilling to give up their stranglehold on Baltic trade. Many of Henry's measures, such as the Navigation Acts and restrictions on the export of raw wool, were partly aimed at hurting the League's trade, but in practice they had little effect. Given the possibility that the League might back one of the Yorkist pretenders to the throne, Henry was probably realistic in not pushing his opposition too far and, by the end of his reign, he had grudgingly accepted that the League had special trading privileges at England's expense.

EXPANDING HORIZONS

In 1492, Ferdinand and Isabella of Spain finally gave their backing to Christopher Columbus' plan to sail westwards in the hope of finding a quick sea passage to the spice-rich Indies. Although not the first voyage of exploration – Portuguese navigators had been inching along the African coast in pursuit of the same goal for some years – it opened European eyes to the possibility of truly international trade. Henry had been approached by Columbus but, in keeping with most of the other rulers in Europe, had turned down his schemes. Nonetheless, Henry was interested in the prospect of exploration and gave his support to John Cabot's efforts to find an accessible westerly route to the Indies. Cabot's voyages led to the possible discovery of Newfoundland in 1496 but also to his death in 1497. Just before his death, Henry renewed his interest by financing Sebastian Cabot's voyage to improve on his father's efforts. Henry's support yielded nothing of tangible value for England, but set the scene for future involvement in the Americas.

The Hanseatic League

In the Middle Ages, a loose association of north German towns and cities had formed to advance their common trading interests in an area that stretched from Russia in the east to Flanders in the west. To do this, they had developed a rudimentary form of 'Common Market', with Lübeck as the principal city and a parliament called the 'Hansetag'. They handled a wide variety of goods, including grain, fish, wax, honey, furs and timber, and imported cloth from the West. By the late fifteenth century, the League was past its peak, but still dominated trade in the rich Baltic Sea region around Sweden and Denmark.

Good surveys of economic development in this period can be found in *Henry VII* by Roger Lockyer and Andrew Thrush (Longman Seminar Studies in History, 1997), and in Caroline Rogers' *Henry VII* (Access to History series, Hodder and Stoughton, 1991).

Royal support for John Cabot

'The king has promised that in the spring Cabot shall have ten ships, armed according to his own fancy, and at his request he has conceded to him all the prisoners, except such as are confined for high treason, to man them with. Vast honour is paid him, and he dresses in silk. The English run after him like mad people, so that he can enlist as many of them as he pleases, and a number of our own rogues besides.'

From a letter written by a Venetian merchant in 1497

THE KEY ISSUES

- What was Henry's attitude towards France?
- How well did he handle the Breton Crisis?

THE KEY SKILLS

Chronology: building an account of events

Interpretation: analysing information to reach conclusions

Evaluation: assessing success and failure

WHAT YOU HAVE TO DO

Given the importance of France in English foreign policy during the Hundred Years War and later, in Henry VIII's reign, it is important to recognise how Henry VII's relations with France fit into the long-standing pattern of conflict, but also how they reflect the new realities of the late fifteenth century.

The Italian Wars

A protracted series of short wars was fought between France, Spain and the Habsburgs between 1494 and 1559 for control of parts of the Italian peninsula. Originally triggered by Charles VIII's ambitions to use the Spanish-held Kingdom of Naples as a springboard for a crusade against the Turks, the action quickly shifted to the north, where the city–state of Milan became vital to France after 1519 as the key to escaping Habsburg encirclement, and to the Habsburgs as a stone in the 'Spanish Road' that linked their sprawling family lands.

England and France

Relations with France had dominated English foreign policy for over a century, but the crushing defeats inflicted on Henry VI and the renewal of France as a self-confident, expansionist power had tipped the balance away from England. A difficult series of choices faced Henry. On the one hand, he owed a personal debt of gratitude to the French king because of the support he had been given in 1485. He also recognised that France had become a major European power, and far outstripped England in wealth and population. Hostile relations did not seem a wise move, especially when pretenders were looking for foreign supporters. However, Henry also had reason to be grateful to Brittany, where he had found shelter for most of his period in exile, but which was a target for French expansion. He also shared the traditional concerns of English kings that if the whole of the cross-channel coastline was dominated by one power, it would place England in a vulnerable position both militarily and in trade.

THE ORIGINS OF THE BRETON CRISIS

At first, Henry sought to ensure peace with France and concluded a series of truces between 1485 and 1489. However, a succession crisis in Brittany, brought on by the rapidly failing health of the duke while his daughter was still a child, quickly created the major foreign policy crisis of Henry's reign. France was keen to absorb neighbouring independent Brittany and proposed a marriage between the duke's daughter and the young French king, Charles VIII. This was refused by Brittany, so French troops were sent in to force the issue. Henry responded cautiously: he sent military help, but insisted in public that this was done without his personal permission, and used his friendship with France to open negotiations to settle the dispute. However, the defeat of the Breton army in July 1488 and the death of the duke escalated the crisis to a new level.

RISING TENSION 1488–1491

Henry tried to rope other countries into his efforts to contain France: he negotiated treaties with Spain (Medina del Campo) and Burgundy, since both were also directly affected by any shifts in French power. He also sought support at home, by summoning Parliament and gaining their approval for a £100 000 grant for a military expedition. In April 1489, an army of modest proportions – estimates vary from 3000 to 6000 – crossed into Brittany. Henry continued to insist to the French that he was not seeking to revive the conquests of his predecessors, but simply looking to protect his country's interests. At first, the operation went well, but the tide quickly turned as the Breton army was again defeated decisively and Spanish and Burgundian support collapsed. Although Henry continued to feed troops into Brittany, he could not prevent the duchess from being forced to marry Charles VIII in December 1491.

THE CLIMAX 1491–1492

The marriage pushed the crisis into its final stage. Henry continued to muster support wherever he could find it: he encouraged Spain, the German princes and even the papacy to get involved. Charles VIII was not likely to take all this activity quietly and he also upped the stakes by receiving Perkin Warbeck at his court. The Breton Crisis reached its climax in the autumn of 1492, when a large English force of 12 000 or so men, led by Henry himself, crossed to the duchy. He was taking an extreme risk: France was militarily stronger, much more familiar with the terrain, closer to its lines of supply and at least as determined as Henry to resolve the problem in its favour. However, Henry gambled that an impressive show of force would convince the French that he meant business and push them to negotiate rather than risk a long war. He was right. Charles VIII had dreams of greater glory in northern Italy, and knew that his marriage to the Duchess of Brittany had given him victory anyway. He had no desire to prolong a war or to wreck his basic friendship with England, which could be valuable in the future. The two countries settled their differences in the Treaty of Etaples in 1492. Henry did surprisingly well, a measure of just how keen Charles was to switch his attention to the riches of Italy. As long as Henry withdrew from Brittany, France would not support his enemies (including Warbeck, who was soon on his travels again) and would even pay for the cost of Henry's expedition.

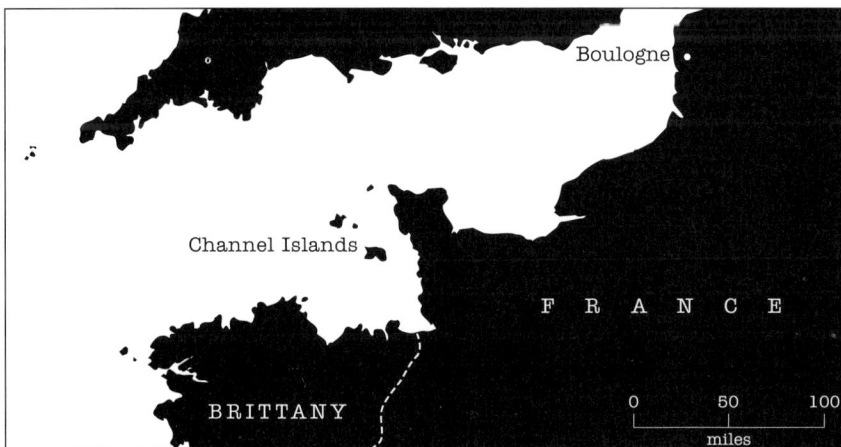

England and Brittany in the later fifteenth century

How was Henry's involvement in France different from that of his predecessors?

Was the outcome of the Breton Crisis brought about by the success of Henry's policies or by a lucky set of circumstances beyond his control?

For a detailed step-by-step account of the Breton Crisis, see pages 76–81 of *Henry VII* by Roger Lockyer and Andrew Thrush (Longman, 1997).

Was the Breton conflict really significant?

Because involvement in the defence of Brittany was Henry VII's only military adventure outside England, it is tempting to give the story of what happened more prominence than it really deserves. It could be argued that the conflict was at best a minor skirmish, a second-rate re-enactment of the glory days of Henry V. The conflict failed to preserve Breton independence (even though the territory was not formally incorporated into the French Crown until 1532) and Henry found it difficult to interest other European rulers in the fate of the duchy. Nonetheless, it does illustrate some of the features of Henry's policies and personality, and you should try to list these in your notes.

THE KEY ISSUES

- What principles governed Henry's relations with other European countries?
- How successfully did he protect and advance England's interests?

THE KEY SKILLS

Interpretation: analysing information to reach conclusions
Evaluation: assessing successes and failures

WHAT YOU HAVE TO DO

Writers have applied a variety of epithets to describe Henry's behaviour, including 'cautious', 'defensive', 'unadventurous', 'realistic' and 'inactive', and are generally agreed that, although unremarkable, his foreign policy was successful, especially given the changes that were under way in the European balance of power at the time. Do you agree? Could Henry have followed a more active military course?

Analysing Henry's foreign policy

Foreign policy is an area in which it is easy to become bogged down in minute detail and miss the larger picture. Don't worry too much about recording all the comings and goings of Henry's diplomacy and military actions when you start making notes. Concentrate instead on our basic questions of *aims*, *methods*, *success* and *impact*, and build in detail as evidence only when you need it. This should help you to avoid falling into the trap of 'telling the story' and should allow you to emphasise your opinions.

International Relations

Henry had a strong need to be involved in European affairs: to win recognition and status, to expand and defend trade interests, but mainly to limit the involvement of other rulers in plots against him. The security of his newly founded dynasty was Henry's overriding concern, and it is therefore unsurprising that virtually every treaty he signed contained clauses that prevented the other party from offering shelter or assistance to his enemies. At the same time, he was also concerned not to overstretch England's limited resources in the face of more powerful foreign states, or to become overly reliant on Parliament for financial aid. This caution dictated his methods. Henry agreed marriage alliances, created commercial links and offered England's friendship and support, but he rarely went to war. This meant that his foreign policy was less spectacular than that of many of his Lancastrian predecessors, but it was realistic given the circumstances.

BURGUNDY

Once a major ally against France in the Hundred Years War, and still a crucial trading partner, relations with Burgundy soured at first under Henry VII. It has been suggested that Henry handled this aspect of foreign policy badly at the beginning of his reign, and that he must shoulder at least some of the blame for the tension that existed until the first decade of the sixteenth century. Either by accident or otherwise, Henry ignored overtures of friendship. He also withdrew special trading privileges that the Yorkist kings had granted to Margaret of Burgundy – again possibly a simple oversight. However, Margaret of Burgundy was Richard III's sister, and a great supporter of the Yorkist cause. Relations between the two countries turned on the extent to which she and Burgundy's ruler, Maximilian, were prepared to support the Yorkist rivals of Henry VII at any moment. Early on, Margaret was willing to provide direct help to the pretenders, and matters came to a head in the early 1490s when she harboured Warbeck. Henry used commercial weapons to threaten Burgundy – he ordered a trade embargo in 1493, despite the damage this might do to English merchants. However, Henry did not pursue a consistently unfriendly policy. He recognised that Burgundy was still a useful counterweight to France across the Channel and was determined to maintain a working relationship, especially after Margaret's death in 1503.

SCOTLAND

The Scots had suffered an uneasy relationship with their English neighbours for centuries and had traditionally used friendship with France as a means of preserving their independence from English aggression. At the start of Henry's reign, Scotland posed no real threat: the assassination of James III in 1488 had led to the succession of the 15-year-old James IV. However, relations became more tense in the 1490s when, during 1495–1497, the Scottish king dabbled in the Warbeck affair by offering the pretender a base and support. It was from this base that Warbeck launched his disastrous invasion of England, and Henry seized the opportunity of his defeat to reach a settlement with James IV in the Truce of Ayton. In 1502, the badly misnamed 'Treaty of Perpetual Peace' was signed, providing for the marriage of Henry's daughter Margaret and James IV as a symbol of the friendship between the two countries. Although it survived the rest of Henry's reign, the truce between England and Scotland soon collapsed under Henry VIII.

SPAIN

England and Spain may have been trade rivals, but they were also natural allies, since both were concerned about the expansion of France. Henry conducted a pro-Spanish policy for much of his reign, symbolised by the Treaty of Medina del Campo, in which the marriage of his oldest son Arthur to Catherine of Aragon was arranged, together with warm promises of mutual support against their enemies. Henry achieved much from his relationship with Spain: treaties and constant diplomatic contacts helped him to overcome the stigma of being a usurper, and Spain never entertained pretenders in the way that other European courts were prepared to do. However, Ferdinand of Aragon was a strong-willed and cunning ruler, and the friendship between England and Spain did not go much more than skin-deep.

Once Ferdinand's wife, Isabella of Castile, had died in 1504, that friendship began to falter. Both Henry and Ferdinand were now looking for new wives and had become rivals in the marriage stakes. Henry had also been frustrated that Ferdinand seemed lukewarm about the proposal that Catherine of Aragon should marry Prince Henry. In the longer term, Ferdinand's uncertain future as ruler of a united Spain made Henry feel that he had become an unsafe bet. For these reasons, he began to regard Isabella's son-in-law, Philip of Burgundy, as a safer prospect. The unexpected arrival of Philip in England in 1506 (his ship was blown off course as he travelled to Spain to claim the crown from Ferdinand) gave Henry the opportunity to tie up a number of loose threads at once. In the Treaty of Windsor, he pressured Philip into returning the Earl of Suffolk, won permission to marry Philip's sister and generally committed England to friendship with Burgundy. These agreements came to nothing, however, because Philip died soon afterwards and Ferdinand assumed full control in Spain. Henry ended his reign facing the realisation that he had unnecessarily insulted Ferdinand and had to repair their relationship.

A historian's classification

Writers dealing with Henry's foreign policy often divide the reign into three phases. S. B. Chrimes, in *Henry VII* (Methuen, 1972) developed this classification in detail:

1 1485–1492, when Henry built a series of truces with his new neighbours and dealt with the Breton Crisis
2 1492–1502, when Henry strengthened England's international presence further by successfully associating himself with Spanish interests, without having to be actively involved in defending them
3 1502–1509, when deaths in his family and the growing importance of the Habsburgs forced Henry into a defensive position

Two broad approaches can be taken to making notes on foreign policy: either country-by-country or chronological. The former method may be best if you wish to avoid the trap of narrative.

A good next step would be to consult Chapter 5 of *Henry VII*, by Jocelyn Hunt and Carolyn Towle (Longman, 1998). They look at the conduct of foreign policy chronologically, using Chrimes' divisions.

1 How did (a) domestic circumstances and (b) wider changes going on in Europe affect Henry's conduct of foreign policy?
2 How consistent were his policies?

THE KEY ISSUES

- How far had monarchy and government changed by 1509?
- What impact did these changes have on Henry VIII's reign?

THE KEY SKILLS

Comparison: identifying similarities and differences
Continuity and change: recognising short- and longer-term effects
Evaluation: reaching an overall verdict

WHAT YOU HAVE TO DO

Historians have placed a great deal of emphasis on 'backwards-referencing'; that is, looking at the extent to which Henry VII continued the work of his Yorkist predecessors rather than reinventing government. You should have some ideas about this from earlier chapters. Now you need to consider the effects of Henry's reign: To what extent did he lay the foundations of the Tudor monarchy? To do this, you need to consider short-term effects and the broader picture of how his reign fits into fifteenth- and sixteenth-century English history.

You could make notes on this chapter thematically, using headings such as Crown, Government, Foreign policy, Culture, Religion and Exploration, or approach these issues chronologically, using headings such as The Situation in 1509, The Situation by the Early Years of Henry VIII's Reign, and The Longer-term Situation.

The Renewal of Government

Henry died on 21 April 1509, and on the next day his only surviving son was proclaimed King Henry VIII. The general mood seems to have been one of muted relief, capturing a hope that the restrictive, unpopular, fearful final years of Henry VII's reign were over and that the 17-year-old Henry VIII would promise a new start. What they overlooked was that this change had only been made possible by the legacy of Henry VII.

THE STABILITY OF THE CROWN

English monarchy was undoubtedly stronger by 1509 than it had been in 1485. Henry VII had restored the reputation and dominance of kingship. Whereas three kings had been deposed in the quarter century before Henry's accession, no monarchs were unseated for a century and a half after it. Simply leaving the throne to his son, who was able to become king to popular acclaim so quickly, was no mean feat in itself. Henry VIII, like his father, had no close relatives to challenge him, but he inherited the same paranoid suspicion of rivals. These were thin on the ground in 1509: the Earl of Suffolk was in prison after being handed back by the Habsburgs – he was executed in 1513 – and his brother Richard was in France. There were no dubious circumstances surrounding the succession for pretenders to play on, and Henry VII had cut through the Yorkist line, disposing of problems along the way. Nonetheless, neither father nor son could ever really believe that they were secure on the throne, and Henry VIII continued to be sensitive to possible threats, however remote, at least until the birth of his son in 1537.

THE POWER OF THE CROWN

More broadly, Henry VII had strengthened the place of the Crown at the centre of the political system. He had reduced the number of key nobles and limited their influence over him. He had put the finances of the Crown back on stable foundations. Government had been focused on the king's person and on his household staff. Parliament remained a useful servant of the king rather than a potential rival. These changes made it possible for Henry VIII to strike a more aggressive pose without having to watch his back constantly. Henry VIII's ability to seize control of the Catholic Church in England after 1534, to asset-strip the great religious houses and to conduct an extreme personal life without any serious backlash from the rest of the ruling elite was a testament to the control that his father had engineered for him.

- What is the difference between the power, authority and image of the Crown?
- Which of these changed most during Henry's reign?

THE IMAGE OF THE CROWN

Historians make great play of the contrast between the miserly reputation that Henry VII has and the lavishness of his court. As far as symbols and imagery are concerned, in some ways Henry looked back to the once-legendary Burgundian court for inspiration, but the beginnings of Tudor splendour – so visible later in Henry VIII's and Elizabeth I's reigns – are to be found in Henry VII's court. As Neville Williams comments, 'Processions, the shouting of royal "vivats", the baring of heads and genuflexions in the royal presence made everyday life seem a heraldic picture in motion.' Henry VII consciously developed the magnificence of courtly life as a way of rebuilding respect for the institution of monarchy, and in this he acted in the same way as his son and grand-daughter were to do in later years.

THE DEVELOPMENT OF GOVERNMENT INSTITUTIONS

By 1509, English government was not so much reformed as set back on the track of development that had been taking place in the later medieval period. Henry had strengthened royal government by showing a close personal interest in the details of policy and by extending the work of household institutions. In the 1490s the 'personalisation' of government went further, with the creation of an inner sanctum, the Privy Chamber – separate from the rest of the court – where the king consulted with only his most trusted advisers. By the end of his reign, Henry had created a sense of remoteness and isolation which, while undoubtedly adding to the mystery of kingship, was not a practice that his son was interested in following, if only because of the difference in their ages.

Henry VIII made immediate changes. He abolished the much-hated Council Learned in Law and executed its leading figures, Dudley and Empson, as scapegoats for its obsession with squeezing money from the nobility. He was also less inclined to become personally involved in all aspects of government, although this did not mean that he handed full control over to others.

As Henry VIII's reign progressed, other changes and additions were made to the structure of government, reflecting new circumstances. The Chamber was put on a proper legal footing early in the reign, confirming its central role in administering royal finances. New financial courts continued to be added to it, especially after the Break with Rome in 1534. Another key change was the development of Parliament. Under Henry VIII, it began to move from the outer edge of the political system and towards the centre, as he began to work with it to add legitimacy to his actions. In the 1530s in particular, his drive to secure a papal divorce from Catherine of Aragon led him to use Parliament regularly, extending the range, scope and volume of legislation to the point at which he became a 'King-in-Parliament' rather than Henry VII's notion of a 'King and Parliament'.

Father and son

A sketch by Holbein of Henry VIII and his father

The powers of later Tudor monarchs

'The king distributes his authority and power in the fashion of five things: in making of laws and ordinances; in making of battle and peace with foreign nations; in providing of money for the maintenance of himself and defence against his enemies; in choosing and election of the chief officers and magistrates; and fifthly in the administration of justice. The first and third are done by the prince in parliament. The second and fourth by the prince himself. The fifth is by the great assize courts.'

Sir Thomas Smith, De Republica Anglorum, 1583

A Forward-looking Land

THE KEY ISSUES

- How had England changed by 1509?
- What impact did these changes have in the short and longer terms?

THE KEY SKILLS

Comparison: identifying similarities and differences
Continuity and change: recognising short- and longer-term effects
Evaluation: reaching an overall verdict

WHAT YOU HAVE TO DO

It was not just politics that changed during Henry VII's reign. Broader shifts in English life and in the status of the country abroad were taking place. To determine the significance of Henry's reign, don't just consider government. Think about society, the economy and religion.

A good brief account of the early years of Henry VIII's reign can be found in Chapter 3 of *The Tudor Years*, edited by John Lotherington (Hodder and Stoughton, 1994). See also Sinclair Atkins, *England and Wales Under the Tudors* (Edward Arnold, 1975).

- How does the fact that Henry VII was 52 years old when he died and Henry VIII only 17 when he succeeded explain the differences in their policies? What other factors could contribute to this explanation?
- Henry VIII has been criticised for the radical changes that he made at the beginning of his reign. How can his actions be justified?

England's relations with its neighbours saw the greatest changes after Henry VII's reign. Between 1485 and 1509 foreign policy had been driven by necessity: lack of money, the shaky succession and the continuing threat from pretenders forced Henry to be circumspect. He had attempted to strike a balance in developing a friendship with Spain while not seeking to be obviously anti-French. This line kept England at peace for much of his reign but, nonetheless, won useful agreements and concessions from the major European powers. Henry VIII, however, completely reversed these policies. In effect, he sought to return English foreign policy to its medieval roots by striking an aggressively anti-French stance. To some extent, he was the willing puppet of Ferdinand of Aragon and Maximilian I: he committed forces to helping Spain take Navarre, despite the lack of any strategic interest in the outcome.

Similarly, in 1513 he began what would be the first of a number of interventions in France by leading 30 000 troops across the Channel as part of a multinational attack on all French frontiers. Again, there were few prizes to be won – Cardinal Wolsey later described the towns that England captured as 'ungracious dogholes'. However, Henry was not simply the pawn of the major powers. As well as asserting his personal prestige, actions abroad were a good distraction for the nobility, who had felt that his father had failed somewhat in his duties as king by not providing them with these sorts of glorious adventures.

One useful offshoot of the revival of an active English foreign policy was the settlement of the Scottish problem. Henry VII had used the defeat of Perkin Warbeck to make a peace with James IV, but this collapsed in 1513 when a Scottish army, egged on by France, invaded northern England. Henry VIII's response was swift and decisive: the Scottish army was destroyed at the Battle of Flodden and James IV and many of his noblemen were killed. By this action, Henry VIII removed the threat from the north for decades.

NEW IDEAS

Henry VII's reign coincided with the height of the European Renaissance and with the famous voyages of Christopher Columbus. The king was interested in both of these developments and began the process of associating England with them. Although his early life had been too disrupted to allow him to develop a thorough appreciation of the arts, Henry nonetheless used royal patronage to encourage writers and artists. In particular, the king became a patron of William Caxton, commissioning the printing of a number of books using newly invented techniques of mass production. He also asked Polydore Vergil to embark on a general history of England. Whereas the typical style of writing to that point had largely focused on creating chronicles, Vergil brought with him the more questioning approach of the Renaissance, to create one of the first analytical accounts of English history. Further afield, in the universities, other writers were starting to be influenced by the principles of humanism – the philosophy that man was not simply directed by God, but had free will and significance as an independent being. It would be too strong to say that Henry laid the foundations of an English Renaissance; his mother's patronage did as much, if not more, in some areas and the impact of new ideas and approaches was patchy and limited, but further developments in Henry VIII's reign definitely sprang from this start.

EXPLORATION

Henry's reign also saw the promotion of overseas exploration, mainly in response to the pioneering voyages of Portuguese and Spanish expeditions. English merchant ships began to venture further into Atlantic waters – trading with the Portuguese island of Madeira, for example – while the court patronised the voyages of John and Sebastian Cabot. However, this immediate interest did not survive Henry's death. In his son's reign, the lack of tangible achievements, the costs of funding ventures at a time of active foreign policy commitments and the problems raised by the possible antagonism of Spain to English rivalry on the oceans convinced the king to pull back. Nevertheless, the long-term ambition of English monarchs to expand their horizons in new directions had its halting start in Henry VII's reign.

THE CHURCH

In the sixteenth century, the problems of the Catholic Church assumed overwhelming importance across western Europe as the Protestant Reformation began. Sinclair Atkins has said of Henry VII that 'nothing in his reign foreshadowed the great clash with the papacy which was to come in Henry VIII's reign'. This is true up to a point: relations between king and Pope remained amicable and, since the clash between Henry VIII and the Pope was more about the political complexities of the royal divorce than about religious doctrine, it was unlikely that Henry VII, with his reputation for scrupulous religious devotion, would cause problems. However, under this calm surface, England had a rich tradition of cynicism about the state of the Church. During Henry VII's reign, John Colet threw off the wealth and personal consumption that seemed to be encouraged by the Catholic Church and returned to the Scriptures for guidance. His teachings, which became very popular at the time, ridiculed medieval thinking and the centuries of nit-picking interpretations that had piled up on the original words of the Bible. His views, like those of others before him, were part of the undercurrent of discontent that boiled over in the sixteenth century, to form the diverse Protestant Reformation.

A woodcut of an early printing press, c. 1500

William Caxton and the development of printing

Caxton began the first printing press at Westminster in 1476. Others quickly sprang up in major population centres, and by 1500 about 360 titles had been printed in England. Many of Caxton's early books were traditional stories of medieval chivalry, but he and others also printed factual texts outlining the form of church services or summaries of the law. Although still expensive, mass production of books brought their price into the range that could be afforded by more than just the wealthy few.

The introduction of printing had two important effects on the development of the English language: first, it led to the standardisation of spelling and the formation of letters; and, second, it helped to broaden vocabulary. Some writers consciously tried to introduce new words into their books, such as Sir Thomas Elyot who, in *The Boke Named the Governour* (1531), used 'accommodate', 'experience' and 'exhaust' for the first time.

Assessment of Henry's reign

The questions posed in this
section are the key issues for the
whole of Henry's reign.
Throughout the chapters dealing
with different aspects of Henry's
work, you have been asked to
consider what his aims, methods,
successes and impact were. You
should already have formed your
own interpretations and ideas
that can be compared against the
suggestions presented here.
Don't worry if you see things
slightly differently: there are no
definite answers, and the
evidence provided about Henry's
reign can sometimes point in
apparently contradictory
directions. What you must be
careful about is to judge Henry
critically but fairly, from the
standpoint of his own times. He
did not introduce democracy or
try to industrialise England, but
these kinds of policies would not
have entered the head of a late
fifteenth-century king. You must
consider how people might have
expected him to behave and what
sorts of decisions were within
the power of a king at this time,
and use these ideas to evaluate
what he did. To give you some
more perspectives, some of the
conclusions reached by various
writers are printed in the
margins of the next few pages.

Synthesis

1. WHAT WERE HENRY'S AIMS?

For someone who was never groomed to be king, and for whom the
chance of taking the crown seemed doubtful–even on the battlefield
at Bosworth–it seems ironic that Henry's principal concern for much
of his later life was to hang on to the title once he had it. The
protection of his fledgling dynasty was always his main priority:
between 1485 and 1489 he created a network of agreements with
other countries and took action at home to establish the legitimacy of
his claim, calm fears and subdue immediate unrest. After 1489, he
remained concerned–even paranoid–about the future. Whereas
most monarchs have the aim of asserting their power and reputation
at the start of their reign, this desire never left Henry. As a usurper
himself, he was fully aware of how momentum against an established
king could build, so he took all threats seriously. After the premature
deaths of his wife and two of his sons, he became ever more
determined to ensure that the Crown was stable and secure, even if
that meant becoming more personally unpopular. Everything else
flowed from this central concern:

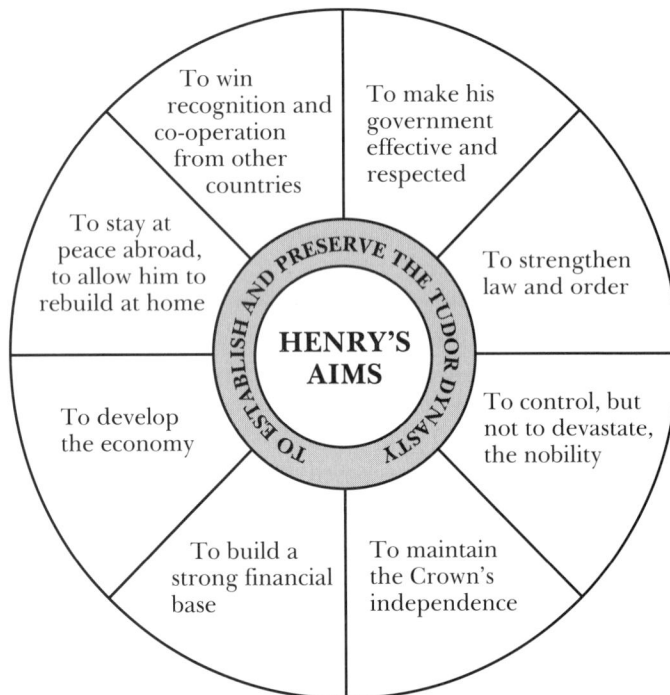

These aims were dictated by circumstances, some of which limited
Henry's freedom of action, while others liberated him from problems
that his predecessors had faced. He was forced, willingly or not, to
follow policies designed to strengthen the Crown by three key factors:

- the nature of his succession, which had disrupted the normal pattern
- the long-term problems of the English state, which had been graphically revealed by the Wars of the Roses
- shifts in the European balance of power

He was helped by:
- the contraction of the nobility, and temporary weaknesses in key families
- the general desire for order and stability
- the re-focusing of European attention on Franco-Spanish rivalry

Circumstances also made Henry inconsistent at times. Within his over-arching aim of protecting the Crown, he changed priorities as necessary to further his ultimate goal.

2. HOW DID HENRY PURSUE HIS AIMS?

To reach his overall objective of a settled monarchy and country, Henry used a combination of legislative, financial and legal tools. His Parliaments created new laws to strengthen the social and economic order and were used to attaint the king's enemies. His use of bonds and recognisances, particularly in the last decade of the reign, and of the more general practice of seeking loans and benevolences, kept the nobility in check by threatening their wealth and status. The Council Learned in Law and other central courts prosecuted the rich, while the powers of Justices of the Peace were strengthened to contain trouble at a local level. In the last resort, Henry also relied on the simple fact that he was the king, and could call on the full range of powers and the innate loyalty that the office commanded. He took great pains at the beginning of his reign to ensure that his title was properly established, and he used the splendour and rich imagery of the monarchy to demand obedience. He was hard-working and had a professional's eye for the detail of government. Unlike Edward IV, he did not try to win over the nobles by handing out lands or building family alliances. His was a much more personal government than others in the fifteenth century, in the sense that Henry monitored closely what was going on and centralised key decision-making power in his own hands. Circumstances again determined his methods. He did not exist in a vacuum: there were already institutions and practices in place by 1485 that worked perfectly well, and Henry inherited many talented officials, whose continued efforts were critical in keeping government going in the shocked atmosphere after the sudden fall of Richard III. Given the almost immediate appearance of rivals and pretenders, Henry did not have the luxury of sitting back to consider how best to run the country. Instead, he adapted and reinforced what was already there, developing forms and procedures as he went along, with no grand plan in mind. Ultimately, these were the methods of a fixer, not an innovator.

The architect of the Tudor monarchy ...

'His achievement was indeed massive and durable. He built his power amid the ruin and ashes of his predecessors. He thriftily and carefully gathered what seemed in those days a vast reserve of liquid wealth. He trained a body of efficient servants. He magnified crown power without losing the co-operation of the commons. He identified prosperity with monarchy. Such was the architect of the Tudor monarchy, which was to lead England out of medieval disorder into greater strength and broader times.'

Sir Winston Churchill, History of the English-Speaking Peoples, volume 2 (Cassell, 1958)

The triumph of stability ...

'Henry was a successful monarch. His reign saw the triumph of stability and realism, but at the cost of a growing number of harsh policies. His techniques were not "modern"; he ran the country on a personal basis as a personal estate.'

David Grossel, in (John Lotherington, editor) The Tudor Years, 1994

Fortunate circumstance ...

'Both through fortunate circumstance and royal policy, Henry came closer to solving the problems of governing England than any of his predecessors had done.'

Alexander Grant, Henry VII, 1985

3. HOW SUCCESSFUL WAS HENRY?

There is general agreement that Henry was a very successful king, if only because the instability that had characterised politics and society for half a century began to fade during his reign. Henry's greatest achievement lay in being able to pass a secure Crown to his son in 1509. In less than 25 years, he had restored peace and prosperity to England and had made the country a respected player in international relations. He had curbed the excessive behaviour of some nobles while retaining their support. He strengthened the machinery of government both locally and at the centre by using existing institutions to their best effect. He established a good working relationship with Parliament, using it to bolster support for his actions and grant much needed taxation, without allowing himself to become too dependent on it. Finances were put on a healthy footing. Henry re-established the solvency of the Crown during the 1490s, and worked hard to ensure that he did not become indebted to other members of the ruling elite. At the time of his death, there was even a small surplus left to kick-start his son's reign. While Henry ruled, commerce flourished. New trade partnerships were founded and by the end of the reign Henry was beginning to look beyond the European horizon.

Yet, there were problems and failures outstanding by 1509. His policies towards the nobility had not simply put them in their place. He had rewarded close friends, loyal servants and family members while refusing to spread his patronage more widely in the manner that was traditional. This provoked resentment and did not resolve the misuse of power by some nobles. Henry compounded this in the last decade of his reign by his ruthless behaviour, and by allowing the sometimes arbitrary actions of his staff. It is not surprising that there was a backlash at the start of his son's reign, seen most visibly in the executions of Dudley and Empson. Henry tried to tackle the ingrained problems created by medieval feudalism, such as retaining, livery and maintenance, but was unable to master them in so short a time. There was still a strong undercurrent of lawlessness and localism, which persisted throughout his reign and despite his efforts. Failure to reform the tax system and a heavy reliance on traditional forms of income left him under-funded compared to his European counterparts, and when he tried to extend direct taxation, two rebellions warned him to pull back. The problems of a post-feudal rural economy were largely ignored or half-heartedly addressed through blunt legislation. Abroad, he failed to contain French ambitions and kept the country determinedly on the sidelines at a time of great change and opportunity.

Should we judge Henry too harshly for these failings? The problems that he faced were often deeply rooted in traditional patterns of behaviour and were beyond the resources of any monarch – especially one constantly distracted by threats to his title – to resolve quickly. Henry was a pragmatist at heart: he tried to straighten out the essentials while accepting that he was working within the limitations of custom and circumstance.

4. WHAT WAS THE IMPACT OF HENRY'S POLICIES?

It is important to distinguish between the person of the monarch and the institution of the monarchy. Henry left the institution in good order; respected and feared. However, his personal reputation suffered at the time and his death was not much mourned by his subjects. During his lifetime, his policies restored the proper balance between the Crown and the rest of the ruling elite, and revitalised the image of English kingship in the eyes of his people and the rest of Europe. In the medium term, his son often chose to steer in a different direction, abandoning the caution of Henry's foreign policy and the tight grip of his financial measures. This did not mean that Henry VII had been wrong, but just that a different king responding to different circumstances needed other alternatives. In the longer term, Henry's lasting impact can be seen. His reign may not have marked a definite break between the medieval and modern worlds, but it contained the seeds of future growth in the interest that Henry showed in exploration, in the greater professionalism of his government and in cultural developments associated with the onset of the Renaissance. Henry established ways of working and expectations of the relationship between ruler and ruled that continued to develop, and still had a resonance in the reign of Elizabeth I a century later.

Was Henry VII's reign a turning-point in English history? By 'turning-point' historians mean that the events of his reign brought about a profound and lasting change, and that these were different from what had come before. Looking broadly, Henry's reign did bring about a political turning-point. Since his reign also coincided with the introduction of printing and the first great wave of European exploration since the Vikings, these also add to the significance of 1485. However, set against this is the lack of change in the economy (the more important developments had taken place over a century earlier, in the aftermath of the Black Death), the Church (where the turning-point came in the mid-sixteenth century, following Henry VIII's Break with Rome) and culture (the slow absorption of Renaissance ideas makes Henry VIII's reign more important). In these aspects, it might be more appropriate to regard Henry's reign as part of a trend, continuing the patterns of development that were already established.

Questionable success ...

'Whether all these actions, the curbing of the magnates and the strengthening of royal government, particularly in financial matters, left the kingdom fundamentally stable remains questionable. Henry VIII's actions on his accession give the impression of a king who wished to conciliate his subjects by easing the pressure on them.'

J. A. F. Thompson, The Transformation of Medieval England (Longman, 1983)

Stern and unpopular ...

'The curbing of aggressive patriotism in foreign affairs and the taming of baronial loutishness at home, by stern and unremitting daily toil, does not bring popularity. Henry was unpopular, especially in his last years of failing health and faltering judgement. He lacked the common touch, the martial glamour, the charisma of the hero; and when he died, consumptive and over-worked, his people were not sorry to see him go.'

E. N. Williams, The Penguin Dictionary of English and European History, 1485–1789 (Penguin, 1980)

A Renaissance monarch ...

'To think of Henry VII as a Renaissance monarch confined within a late medieval setting is to come close to an understanding of the significance of his reign.'

Roger Lockyer and Andrew Thrush, Henry VII, 1997

Argument

1. WHY WAS HENRY VII ABLE TO SEIZE THE CROWN IN 1485?

About this question

At first glance, it seems very straightforward, but you have to make some important decisions about what you think it is asking about. Is it just about the events of 1485, particularly the Battle of Bosworth Field? Is it just about what Henry did to win the crown in 1485? Both of these raise valid ideas, but are too narrow on their own – you also need to consider the longer-term developments that propelled Henry towards the throne and what actions his enemies took. This will enable you to create a better explanation, because it will have a greater range of points and ideas.

The question can be answered most logically by replying 'because ...' and then giving a series of reasons. This makes it a 'list-type' essay. To keep the structure clear for the reader, put each reason in a separate paragraph, with a sentence at the start that includes the factor that you are going to write about.

Essay plan

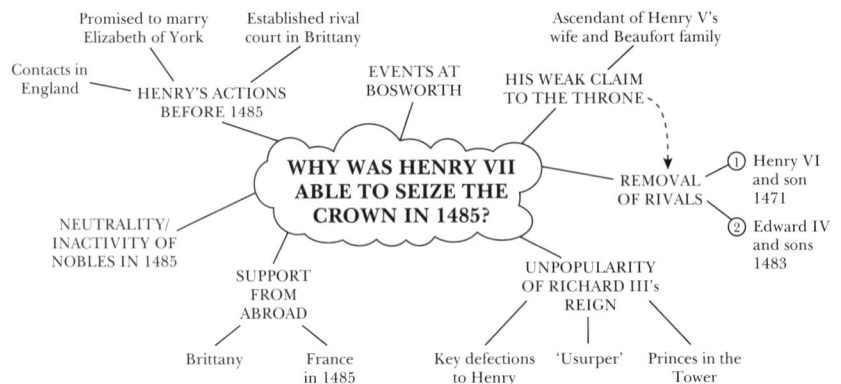

How to improve your answer

Not all of the factors shown in the plan are of equal importance. For instance, you might argue that even though Henry's rivals disappeared one after another between 1467 and 1485, this was not enough to win him the crown if Richard III and the remaining Yorkists were secure, and so the unpopularity of Richard is more important. In this way, you could arrange the factors in your explanation in order of importance, giving your reasons as you go along. It does not matter whether you start at the most important reason and work down or begin the other way. Alternatively, you could think about grouping factors into (1) those that relate directly to Henry's strengths and (2) those that illustrate his enemies' weaknesses. Then, in your conclusion, you could assess which of these groups was more important. In either case, what you are doing is going beyond simply listing reasons at random: you are moving towards creating an overall argument, which shows that you can debate the answer in a more complex way.

2. WAS HENRY VII EVER IN SERIOUS DANGER OF LOSING THE CROWN AFTER 1485?

About this question

Whereas the last question required you to think up a list of reasons to explain something, this one poses a different sort of challenge: it wants you to discuss an idea. In a **discussion-type** essay, you need to remember that examiners are not just looking for range of ideas, but also for balance of argument. You will not do well if you just use the answer to voice your personal opinions, because these are likely to be one-sided and incomplete. Instead, you need to plan carefully to create a 'Yes' and 'No' argument, each aspect of which should contain a variety of points. Here are some ideas to get you started.

Essay plan

Introduction: say where the threats to Henry's crown came from. Mention Lovell, Simnel, Warbeck and Suffolk. Comment that, to Henry, each posed a threat that could not be ignored, but that this is not necessarily the same as a 'serious' threat (which suggests that they could have realistically unseated him).

Yes	No
Lambert Simnel	
• The threat came at the start of the reign – Henry could not be sure of support	• The claim was based on the Earl of Warwick, who was still alive but in prison – Henry paraded the earl to undermine support
• The threat came shortly after Lovell's attempt to stir rebellion	• Unequal forces at the Battle of Stoke – Henry was well-prepared
• There was support from Ireland, where Simnel was crowned king	• The decisive outcome of the battle weakened the Yorkist cause (for example, death of Lincoln)
• There was support from Burgundy	
• There were links to the Yorkist claimant, the Earl of Lincoln	
• Invasion of England and pitched battle	
Perkin Warbeck	
• There was broader support, from France, Ireland, Scotland and Burgundy at various times	• But in each case it was temporary support (for example, France abandoned Warbeck in the Treaty of Etaples)
• Revelation of traitors at the heart of the court – this forced a reappraisal of government, including the development of the Privy Chamber	• There was no link between Warbeck and the Cornish rebels
• The threat coincided with the Cornish Rebellion	• The invasion attempt was disastrous
Other claimants	
• The threat from Edmund de la Pole – worsened by the deaths of Elizabeth of York and two sons in 1500–1502	• No invasion – handed over in negotiations between Henry VII and Philip of Austria

Writing an introduction

Introductions serve a number of purposes (although which ones depends on the precise question), so knowing what these are can help you to see what you need to write:

• to show the reader that you have understood the question
• to define key words and ideas included in the question
• to set out the overall shape of the answer as a quick guide for the reader
• gently to move the reader into the main part of the answer

Common problems such as over-long or irrelevant introductions stem from ignoring these purposes.

Here are two opening paragraphs to question 1. To judge which is better, ask yourself which comes closest to meeting the purposes of an introduction:

'Henry VII became king of England in August 1485 when he defeated and killed Richard III at the Battle of Bosworth Field (although the actual site of the battle may have been somewhere else). In the battle, Richard's forces rushed towards Henry's position, nearly reaching him, but the timely intervention of Sir William Stanley's army swung the victory Henry's way.'

'Henry VII became king of England through a combination of careful planning and simple good fortune. Although he had a claim to the throne and busily planned for the possibility in the 1480s, it was the weaknesses of his Yorkist enemies that positioned him as a king-in-waiting by August 1485.'

Whether you are writing a homework essay or a timed answer in an exam, careful planning is essential if you are to produce your best work. Plans need not be long, and should take no more than about five minutes to write in timed conditions, but they should be sufficient to summarise how you are going to approach the question and show what points should go where. They can be diagrams (as in question 1), tables (as in question 2) or notes (as in question 4): it does not matter as long as it is clear.

The advantages of devoting a few minutes at the start of a timed essay to planning it out are as follows:

- Planning can help you to check that you have enough points to answer the question satisfactorily. As a rule of thumb, if you cannot think of more than five key arguments, you will probably score low marks, and should look for another possible essay.
- It can help you to avoid a jumbled answer, where there seems to be no overall structure or logic to the paragraphs.
- It will allow you to organise points so that they can be presented with the greatest impact.
- It will enable you to write more quickly: you will know what to write next and so you should find that you are not interrupting your writing too often to have to think through a new paragraph.

How to improve your answer

The real key to this question lies in the word 'serious'. What you need to do is to show that there might have been possible problems but that these were magnified by Henry's own insecurity, which made threats seem more real than they in fact were. There was probably little actual danger that Henry would lose the crown, because:

- rebels found little support in England – the appetite for political instability seemed to have largely disappeared (even Henry saw this when trying to muster support during his invasion in 1485)
- serious rivals around whom support could collect, such as the Earl of Warwick, were quickly imprisoned
- marriage alliances and skilful diplomacy blocked off foreign support
- Henry's intelligence network alerted him to problems quickly, before they got out of hand

But what also matters is Henry's *perception* of the problem. There were a number of factors that made him feel sensitive to threats:

- he had little experience of kingship – or of England – at the start of the reign
- he offered few rewards to the nobility and did not act like a typical medieval king
- both Scotland and Ireland harboured his enemies, keeping them perilously close to the English borders
- rivalry persisted for most of the reign, creating a continuing unsettled atmosphere
- Henry was a usurper himself, and could appreciate the potential threat that enemies working from foreign bases might pose

3. BY WHAT MEANS, AND TO WHAT EXTENT, HAD HENRY VII RESTORED ROYAL AUTHORITY BY 1509?

About this question

You will see that there are, in fact, two questions being asked: 'by what means' (or 'how') and 'to what extent'. The first part is another form of 'list-type' question, demanding a series of ways in which Henry put the Crown back in control. The second part is more complex (and so would probably carry more marks in the examiner's mind): it is a discussion-type question that asks for an argument about Henry's achievements. By referring to 'extent', the question is opening up a number of possibilities, ranging from the view that Henry had totally restored royal authority to the complete opposite, that he had absolutely failed. The truth, as usual, is somewhere in the middle, so you need to show that Henry had definite achievements, but also left unfinished business for his successors.

To organise the answer, then, you need to do three things:
1. explain what his methods were
2. show that they were successful, and
3. show that there were limitations

You could either write this up as a three-part essay, or – because there might be repetition between these sections – discuss the successes and limitations of each method straight after you have explained it. This has the advantage of keeping material on the same theme together in one place, making it easier to follow and generally producing a more tightly argued answer.

Essay plan

Means	Achievement	Problems
1. Establishment of his claim to rule		
• Marriage to Elizabeth of York • Parliamentary recognition • Rewards for loyalty	• Quickly overturned doubts about the legitimacy of his claim • Marriage aimed to heal differences between Lancaster and York	• Unwillingness to use land and titles as rewards left some (Edmund de la Pole, for example) feeling undervalued • Difficulties with rivals throughout reign
2. Firm personal control over government		
• Direct involvement in financial matters • Control of privilege • Use of household as focus of government • Development of Privy Council in the 1490s	• Probably had tighter control than any other king before him • Helped to strengthen reputation of Crown as hard-working and in control • Restricted opportunities for others to build power bases in government	• Became a more remote figure in latter years of reign – encouraged factionalism? • Achievement depended on having the right temperament – Henry VIII did not share his father's diligence
3. Strengthening of the image of the monarchy		
• Royal progress in 1486 • Lavishness of court – promotion of the arts, Richmond Palace • Coinage	• Fostered an image of a sumptuous court with king firmly at the centre and of the 'mystique' of monarchy	• But not a typical medieval king – his more cautious approach did not offer nobility personal glory • Last years of reign damaged his personal reputation (but Henry VIII welcomed in 1509)
4. Financial pressures on unruly subjects		
• Bonds and recognisances • Loans and benevolences	• Range of noblemen placed under financial obligations • Extent of individual fines (for example, Earl of Northumberland) • Thoroughness of collection	• Hostility to methods of enforcement – through Council Learned in Law • Hostility to excessive use after 1502 • Resentment meant that Council could not have been used as a long-term strategy • Backlash at start of Henry VIII's reign
5. Improvement of law and order in local communities		
• Strengthened role of JPs • Laws dealing with illegal retaining • Changes to methods of organising regional government • Development of legal system	• Reduction of noble 'spheres of influence' that had built up under the Yorkists • Less illegal retaining	• Retaining continued • 'Over-mighty nobility' remained, but fewer in number • Undercurrent of lawlessness remained – rebellions in Yorkshire and Cornwall against government policy
6. Restriction of other members of the ruling elite		
• Limited use of Parliament • Greater use of professional bureaucrats	• Parliament not allowed to challenge royal authority as in earlier reigns • Use of administrators loyal to king – for example, John Morton	• Still reliant on co-operation of nobility and Parliament to pursue policies

Structuring paragraphs

At A-level, you should try to avoid narrative – just telling the story of what happened – at all costs. Examiners will assume that you know basic details, and will be looking for your use of this information to present a reasoned argument. One way to avoid narrative is to organise your paragraphs around ideas rather than facts. So, the first sentence of each paragraph should identify the issue or argument that you wish to develop. In question 3, for example, you might begin one of the paragraphs with 'One important way in which Henry restored royal authority was through his firm personal control of government.' This then gives you something to explain and expand in the next few sentences, and you can introduce facts at this point to illustrate what you are saying. When you are beginning to write formal essays, you might find it useful to use one colour for arguments and another for facts, so that you can keep a check on the balance between them. Ideally, you should have arguments appearing regularly, with facts following for a couple of lines at most.

Making connections

One useful trick when writing paragraphs is to have a stock of words and phrases that you can use to join different arguments together. This will improve the flow of your writing and allow you to establish relationships between the ideas you are presenting. Examples of these linking words are:

However ...   Additionally ...
So ...   But ...
Moreover ...   Nonetheless ...
Therefore ...

What do examiners want?

All examination boards publish annual reports, which are written by examiners and give information such as the ways in which students tackled questions, common mistakes, which answers were most popular and the overall performance of the year group. They also give mark schemes, which show how examiners think the questions should have been answered. Where possible, you should consult these for ideas about the precise expectations of the exam board setting your papers. However, all history essays need to demonstrate the same basic skills, whatever the question or exam board:

- **relevance** to the question set – every year, examiners complain bitterly that their careful efforts in choosing the particular wording and angle of a question are ignored by candidates who just launch into pre-prepared answers
- a **balanced** response – looking at all facets of the answer, not just a few aspects or one side of the overall argument
- a **range** of ideas and arguments – offering multiple factors or a series of discussion points, not just one or two ideas
- **depth** of illustration – selecting enough precise factual knowledge to support the arguments being put forward (and not the other way around!)
- **clear presentation** – a formal written style, good grammar and accurate spelling

How to improve your answer

The points raised in the plan will go a long way to answering the question, but you could take the essay further by stepping back from all these ideas and reaching some **general** conclusions about Henry's achievements. To do this, try to summarise what you think the 'authority' of the Crown was in 1485 and in 1509, and then compare the two statements.

4. 'THE INTERESTS OF DYNASTIC SECURITY OVERRODE ALL OTHER CONSIDERATIONS.' IS THIS A FAIR ASSESSMENT OF HENRY VII'S FOREIGN POLICY?

About this question

Again, think about the basic question type, so that your planning immediately takes shape. This question does not need a 'list-type' answer, because it does not a provoke a 'because ...' response. Instead, it is another variation on a discussion type. This time, one factor – 'the interests of dynastic security' – has been given special prominence, and you are being asked to judge whether it was the most important consideration in foreign policy. So, you need a 'Yes'/'No' approach again, with a variety of arguments in each half. The focus on just one factor raises two further questions: Was it the most important consideration in the dealings that Henry had with each of the countries you have looked at? Was it constantly his most important interest, or can you detect changes of emphasis? Answering either of these questions could give you different ways of planning the whole essay.

Essay plan 1

- *Introduction.* What is meant by the key phrase 'the interests of dynastic security'? You could mention limiting support for pretenders, associating his family with other European monarchies through marriage, and strengthening the safety of English frontiers.
- *Main part of the essay.* Take each of the countries that England had dealings with and consider what Henry's aims were, and whether dynasticism was the key:
  - France: mention the problem of Brittany and the contents of the Treaty of Etaples.
  - Burgundy: include Margaret of Burgundy's willing support for Simnel and Warbeck, Henry's willingness to undermine trade interests in the mid-1490s – the embargo – and, when faced with the possible collapse of Spanish unity after 1504, his efforts to win over Philip of Burgundy in the Treaty of Windsor, while still pursuing trade advantages in the 'Malus Intercursus'.
  - Spain: mention the various policy aims displayed in the Treaty of Medina del Campo – such as the marriage agreement and trade terms – and Henry's interest in supporting the Cabots, even

though they were threatening Spanish seafaring interests. Also consider Henry's partial abandonment of the pro-Spanish policy after 1504.

- – Scotland: explain why the Scots were seen as a threat to Henry's security and how the Truce of Ayton and 'Perpetual Peace' tried to neutralise the problem.
- *Conclusion*. Summarise the variety of aims that Henry pursued and argue where 'dynastic security' comes in this list.

Essay plan 2

Alternatively, start from a chronological approach and explore the consistency of Henry's aims:

- *Introduction*. Use the same opening as plan 1. Refer to S. B. Chrimes' argument that Henry's foreign policy can be divided into three phases.
- *1485–1492*. Outline the various treaties that Henry signed to ensure recognition of his dynasty and consider the Breton Crisis. What issues were at stake?
- *1492–1502*. Explain the impact of Perkin Warbeck on Henry's dealings with Burgundy in this period and mention the support given to John Cabot. Discuss why good relations with Scotland were important for dynastic security and how Henry tried to improve them when the chance arose in 1497.
- *1502–1509*. Refer to the rapid changes in diplomacy brought about by the deaths of close family members and Isabella of Castile. Link these to Henry's search for a wife for himself and his remaining son, and to misguided efforts to back Philip of Burgundy in 1506. Bring in the 'Malus Intercursus' as an example of continuing interest in trade and Henry's support for Sebastian Cabot in his final year as king.
- *Conclusion*. Summarise the variety of aims that Henry pursued and argue whether the search for 'dynastic security' was followed consistently throughout his reign.

How to improve your answer

Both of these plans will create a thorough answer to the question, but to gain high marks the idea of priorities needs to come across strongly. It would be possible to argue that dynastic security really was the most important aim, because:

- all of Henry's other foreign policy aims stemmed from this one objective (including the promotion of trade, since a strong economy helped domestic stability)
- he pursued this aim throughout the reign – it can be seen in his negotiation of truces immediately after he had become king, and in his efforts to re-marry himself and his son in his last years
- he pursued this aim in his dealings with all other countries

Writing a conclusion

Conclusions give you the opportunity to draw together the threads of your answer. There are different schools of thought about what makes a good conclusion, but in general, they should be short (no more than three or four sentences) and could:

- summarise the main arguments of the answer (which is especially useful if you think your answer has not been clear in places, or simply to make sure that the reader has got the point of what you wanted to say)
- put forward a personal view of the answer (discussion-type questions in particular seem to invite your view once you have presented all the different arguments on both sides)
- give the answer impact by offering a contentious or dramatic perspective

Putting pen to paper

The worst essays are those written in a hurry. Ideally, you should take the time between when the essay is set and when it is due in to plan, reflect and refine:

- Start by planning your answer soon after it is set.
- Come back to it after a break and review it, adding anything else you have remembered.
- Write the essay in rough.
- Come back to it after a break and review it. Try reading it aloud to see if it makes sense grammatically as well as historically. If you think there is a problem, show some or all of it to your teacher.
- Once you are satisfied, write it up (or, even better, word process and then spell-check it). Leave yourself time to read it through and make final corrections.

Final Review

The Review section is like a conclusion to an essay: it brings together some of the information and arguments presented in this book and offers some final ideas for looking at the topic.

This diagram summarises the reign of Henry VII. Whereas the rest of this book has been thematic, with each chapter looking at different topics and issues, the focus here is chronological. Listing events in the order in which they happened allows us to make connections between the different strands of Henry's reign, such as foreign and domestic policies or government and the economy.

The value of chronology

'Change in one theme may have taken place at a different rate than in another but contemporaries did not necessarily separate them in practice: religion, domestic policy and foreign affairs were inextricably linked for many Englishmen.'
Richard Brown and Christopher Daniels, Learning History: a Guide to Advanced Study (Macmillan, 1986)

From the placing of the information on these pages, it would seem that Perkin Warbeck posed the central problem of Henry's reign. Do you agree?

SECURITY OF THE CROWN AT HOME
- Coronation Oct. 1485
- First session of Parliament Nov. 1485
- Imprisonment of Warwick 1485
- Marriage to Elizabeth of York Jan. 1486
- Royal progress 1486
- Birth of Prince Arthur Sept. 1486

THE END OF THE WARS OF THE ROSES
- Battle of Bosworth Field Aug. 1485
- Lovell's uprising Mar. 1486
- Lambert Simnel June 1486 –June 1487
- Battle of Stoke June 1487

WINNING RECOGNITION ABROAD
- Truce with Scotland Oct. 1485
- Treaty with Maximilian Jan. 1487
- Medina del Campo Mar. 1489
- Treaty with Portugal 1489
- Trade agreement with Denmark 1489

BRETON CRISIS
- French invasion and defeat of Breton army 1487–1488
- Marriage of Anne of Brittany to Charles VIII Dec. 1491
- English invasion of France Oct. 1492
- Treaty of Etaples Nov. 1492

A summary of the reign of Henry VII

POPULAR PROTESTS

orkshire rebellion 1489
ornish rebellion 1497

IRELAND

- Removal of Kildare 1492
- Poynings' Law Dec. 1494

PERKIN WARBECK

- First appearance in Ireland Nov. 1491
- Travelled to France 1492
- Then to Burgundy and Austria 1493
- Then to Scotland 1496
- Invasion and arrest in Cornwall 1497
- Plots and execution 1499

SCOTLAND

- Truce of Ayton 1497
- Perpetual Peace 1502
- Marriage of Princess Margaret to James IV 1503

BURGUNDY

- Trade embargo 1493
- Magnus Intercursus Feb. 1496

REFORM OF GOVERNMENT

- Execution of Sir William Stanley Feb. 1495
- Emergence of the Privy Council system mid-1490s
- Creation of Council Learned in Law mid-1490s

FAMILY TRAGEDIES

- Death of Prince Edmund 1500
- Death of Prince Arthur 1501
- Death of Elizabeth of York 1503
- Death of Cardinal Morton 1500

CHANGING DIPLOMACY

- Death of Isabella of Castile 1504
- Treaty of Windsor 1506
- Malus Intercursus 1506
- Death of Philip of Burgundy 1506
- Sebastian Cabot 1509

RUTHLESS GOVERNMENT?

- Bonds and recognisances 1502–1509
- Law against illegal retaining 1504
- Search for a new wife 1503–1509
- Collision with Spain 1504–1509

From the way in which this diagram has been presented, it is possible to reach a number of conclusions:

- There were three stages to Henry's reign:
  - the end of the Wars of the Roses, 1485–1489
  - the threat of Perkin Warbeck, 1491–1499
  - family tragedies and their consequences, 1500–1509
- Foreign and defence policies were not separate realms, but closely related.
- Henry's aims and preoccupations changed as the reign progressed, although his objective of strengthening the Crown and his dynasty remained constant.
- Henry's policies were driven by insecurity. For instance, the appearance and activities of Perkin Warbeck influenced his policies towards Ireland, the reform of government and relations with European states.

This diagram is one representation of Henry's reign – others are certainly possible. For instance, you could separate out the different strands of the reign, such as Government, Foreign Policy, Stability, Finances and The Economy, and use these as column headings for a timeline. Alternatively, you could put the years of Henry's reign down the middle of a page and use two columns – one to either side – to map out evidence of growing stability and continuing instability.

Where next?

This book is part of a series called 'Pathfinder' because it gives you an introduction to Henry VII's reign and maps out a way through the topic that will help you to tackle the more detailed textbooks on this subject confidently. Once you have used the information and ideas presented here to get started on researching the topic, you should do the following:

- Consult other books on Henry VII to find answers to specific questions that you have, or to add more depth to your knowledge of some aspects of the reign. A number have been suggested in earlier chapters, and all are excellent at taking you further into the topic:

  Alexander Grant, *Henry VII: the Importance of his Reign in English History* (Routledge Lancaster Pamphlets, 1985)

  Jocelyn Hunt and Carolyn Towle, *Henry VII* (Longman History in Depth, 1998)

  Roger Lockyer and Andrew Thrush, *Henry VII*, 3rd edn (Longman Seminar Studies in History, 1997)

  Caroline Rogers, *Henry VII* (Access to A-level History, Hodder and Stoughton, 1991)

- Look at past essay questions for the syllabus you are studying, and try to apply what you know to planning answers to some of them.

- Talk to other students about Henry VII and compare your ideas and conclusions. History is a subject built on argument and debate, so you will probably find a variety of opinions – discussing them will help you to express, check and defend your views.

This book has been about a remarkable, but shadowy, figure who successfully re-imposed royal government in England during a turbulent century. To the modern world, Henry is a largely forgotten figure, eclipsed by the reigns of Richard III and Henry VIII. Unlike these kings, he had no remarkable personal characteristics, fought no spectacular wars and suffered no major defeats. Instead, he was a competent and efficient king with a tinge of necessary ruthlessness, a man to be respected but not liked.

Henry had a distant claim to the throne, which was advanced by a series of dynastic accidents rather than by a grand plan to become king. He capitalised on Richard III's weaknesses to make a bid for the crown in 1485 and was able to seize it in another twist in the Wars of the Roses. He quickly emphasised his rightful claim to the throne, but this alone did not guarantee that he would remain king for long. Instead, it was his realistic, cautious, opportunist and ruthless approach to government that secured the English crown on the heads of the Tudors. Henry took what was already there and moulded it to his needs and ways of working. He was no great innovator, but he was a good manager of existing resources. His greatest successes at home lay in restoring the reputation of the English monarchy as a stable institution, respected by the ruling elite and strong enough to resist the forces of instability. Although the Tudor monarchy reached the heights of its splendour in the courts of Henry VIII and Elizabeth I, it was built on the sturdy foundations laid between 1485 and 1509. It is easy to over-dramatise what Henry did, and to become seduced by romantic images of his long path to the throne and his heroic defence against evil pretenders and enemies of the kingdom, but the actuality is probably much more mundane. Henry often merely reacted to circumstances, and spent much of his reign immersed in the endless grind of winning obedience to royal wishes. He was constantly watchful and exhibited a mistrustfulness that sometimes bordered on paranoia.

Was Henry's Reign a Turning-Point?

Henry VII has not attracted the same interest or heated debates that characterise the way in which historians have approached other Tudor monarchs. In part, this is because there was a near-universal acceptance of 1485 as the start of the modern era and of Henry himself as a so-called 'New Monarch'. In the 1970s and 1980s, however, writers began to challenge these assumptions and offer revisionist interpretations that looked more closely at how the reign fitted into the context of what had gone before. New interpretations of the Wars of the Roses also pushed historians towards the view that Henry's methods and interests were similar to those of Edward IV and earlier kings, downgrading the importance of 1485. For some historians, however, the feeling that the pendulum has swung too far against regarding Henry's reign as significant has led to efforts to emphasise that he was not merely a clone of Edward IV but made a crucial impact in his own right. Views of the period have also been affected by the direction from which the historian is looking. Traditionally, Henry's reign was viewed from the perspective of the Later Tudors, so he seemed to be the originator of the powerful state that emerged in the sixteenth century. Some writers, however, have looked forwards towards the reign from a medieval starting point, and have recognised continuities in the nature of government and the problems it faced.

Continuities	Changes
• Henry emphasised his links with the past through marriage and family • He relied on the nobility as instruments of government – 'over-mighty' subjects were quieter, but still remained • He followed Edward IV's policies of attacking retaining and lawlessness • Traditional sources of income – including feudal dues – were retained, although exploited more fully • The financial machinery established by Edward IV continued to be used • There was further development of a professional group of administrators to conduct business • Henry restricted use of Parliament as far as possible • There was no great change in the relationship with the Church	• A new, stable dynasty – which ruled from 1485 to 1603 – and the defeat of the Yorkist line • The end of the open conflict of the previous generation – disputes among members of the ruling elite now tended to become 'institutionalised', and were fought out at court between different factions rather than on the battlefield • There was less of a partnership with the nobility – titles and rewards were restricted, in a different method to Edward IV's 'inclusive' policies • The style of the monarchy was more remote and 'business-like' • Aggressively anti-French policies that had dominated the Hundred Years War were abandoned, and there was a shift to a more cautious policy of balance and containment • Overseas exploration was promoted • The influence of the Renaissance and of humanist learning grew steadily

This book has tried to chart a course that draws on these different approaches. Among the arguments that have been used are the following:

- That Henry's reign retained strong links to the past, especially to the second reign of Edward IV (1471–1483)
  - *but* that there were important developments, especially in the form and style of government, that created a powerful new legacy for his son and grandchildren.
- That Henry tried to tackle the deep political problems that had built up over the past generation
  - *but* that he was less successful in devising solutions than a quick glance might reveal.
- That he was helped by favourable circumstances and sheer good fortune
  - *but*, nonetheless, that he possessed strong personal qualities that helped him to be the right man at the right moment in English history.

By using these differing perspectives, we can move beyond simply describing what happened between 1485 and 1509, to form a much richer and more complex understanding of what was once routinely dismissed as a worthy, but dull, period of history – and we can begin to understand Henry as a three-dimensional human being, rather than as a distant, often forgotten, character in the long procession of monarchs.

Knowledge and skills

By the time your study of Henry VII is completed, not only should you have picked up a wide body of knowledge, but you should also have begun to develop useful skills that can be applied throughout your history course. You will find that the main themes of this book:

- dealing with rivals and uncertainty
- developing government
- raising income
- expanding trade
- managing other members of the ruling elite, such as Parliament and the nobility
- relations with France and Spain

are all universal themes that can be applied to any of the Tudor monarchs you might go on to study. The only key strand that is missing is religion and the Church, which becomes important from the reign of Henry VIII onwards.

Equally, you will have developed some skills related not just to study but also to historical research, that should be applied to whatever you are looking at:

- note-making techniques
- time management
- using a variety of resources
- essay-writing skills
- reading skills
- locating relevant information
- selecting information
- presenting information
- identifying facts and opinions
- creating an argument
- using primary evidence

These are among the skills that will help you not only to get a good grade in this subject, but to work more effectively in your later life.

Index